Praise for *Deep Learning:*
Engage the World Change the World
by Michael Fullan, Joanne Quinn,
and Joanne McEachen

This book elevates deep learning from an instructional tool to a systemic approach designed to create powerful synergies to enhance professional, social, and cultural capital. It is built on the deep belief that all students can learn if school systems shift from sorting talent, where only a minority of winners cross the finishing line, to developing the talent of diverse learners. *Deep Learning*'s power lies in providing practical advice to help school systems evolve, for rules to become guidelines, and ultimately, for good practice to become culture.

Andreas Schleicher, *Special Advisor on Education Policy to OECD's Secretary-General and Director of PISA*

We live in a world where creativity is our new capital. Michael Fullan, Joanne Quinn, and Joanne McEachen's book takes us deeply into this world. Read, launch, and learn!

Daan Roosegaarde, *Dutch Designer, Architect, and Innovator*

Drawing upon decades of hard-fought education experience and with an eye toward our precarious future, Michael Fullan, one of the world's most respected education experts, along with co-authors Joanne Quinn and Joanne McEachen, has written a comprehensive and practical guide on school transformation. Intended for both policy makers and practitioners, the book toggles between theory and practice to deconstruct the "how" of education system change. It is a must-read for anyone who is serious about preparing our children for the complex, interdependent world they will inherit.

Barbara Chow, *Former Education Director, William and Flora Hewlett Foundation*

Michael Fullan, Joanne Quinn, and Joanne McEachen offer a powerful set of ideas to enable deeper learning on a large scale. Deep learning develops examples at every level of the system— from the individual student and teacher to the classroom, school, and state—suggesting how learning may be radically redesigned in ways that could change schooling as we know it.

Linda Darling-Hammond, *President, Learning Policy Institute, and Charles E. Ducommun Professor Emeritus, Stanford University*

There are many "deeper teachers," some "deeper schools," but very few "deeper systems." For that reason, we are very lucky that Michael Fullan, Joanne Quinn, and Joanne McEachen have channeled their prodigious talents for identifying the right levers for systems change to deeper learning. Drawing on their work with 1,200 schools in seven countries, they describe concretely what powerful learning looks like for both students and adults, and how system leaders can support the creation of challenging, engaging, and empowering learning for all students. Every system leader who wants to transform their system from an industrial era bureaucracy to a modern learning organization should read this book!

Jal Mehta, *Associate Professor, Harvard Graduate School of Education*

This book takes us on an exciting journey exploring why and how to deepen learning, and in so doing enables the teaching profession to rediscover the joy of teaching, and immerses students in the endless universe of learning.

Lynn Davie, *Director, Learning and Teaching Branch,*
Secondary Reform, Transitions and Priority Cohorts Division,
Department of Education and Training, Victoria, Australia

This book is a call for action. Michael Fullan, Joanne Quinn, and Joanne McEachen take us on a journey of change based on deep conceptual knowledge and vast experience of practice. Drawing on work from seven countries around the world, *Deep Learning* shows the humanistic and international spirit of the DL movement.

Miguel Brechner, *President, Plan Ceibal, Uruguay*

Once again, Michael Fullan and his colleagues, Joanne Quinn and Joanne McEachen, have produced a groundbreaking book that explores how to make more profound learning experiences available to a broad range of students. For educators interested in furthering equity and tapping into the intrinsic curiosity of students, this book will be an invaluable resource.

Pedro A. Noguera, *PhD, Distinguished Professor of Education,*
UCLA Graduate School of Education and Information Studies

Deep Learning will become your mantra for giving your students a sense of purpose and connectedness to the world. Recently I witnessed deep learning in action at the authors' recent international gathering. The teachers were on fire. Their commitment to teaching had been re-ignited by the focus on engaging students who no longer saw school as relevant to their lives. Students demonstrated a strong sense of identity and creativity, mastery, and engagement. This book shows us how successful our students can be!

Alan November, *Senior Partner, November Learning*

Deep Learning is a book that pulls the cover away from the game of schooling and highlights the need for systemwide changes to ensure that every student becomes empowered and passionate as part of their own learning process. *Deep Learning* brings together the work of practitioners from around the world, as they share concrete examples of revitalized classrooms, schools, and entire districts. Ultimately the book shows how the transformation of learning in schools and districts can result in both excellence and equity for all students in today's global and digital world.

Tom D'Amico, *Associate Director of Education,*
Ottawa Catholic School District Board

Deep Learning: Engage the World Change the World addresses the missing learning momentum we need so that students, educators, and parents carry on learning beyond school. With this deep learning mindset, as new truths and contexts emerge and new competencies are required, we will all be equipped to master them.

Patrick Miller, *Ontario School Principal*

Deep Learning: Engage the World Change the World provides insight into the potential when we keep the student experience at the center of our thinking. When we create conditions that engage teachers and learners in a reciprocal relationship, the outcomes are not only higher achievement and wellbeing, but also the door is opened to begin to address historic inequities for some groups of students.

Cathy Montreuil, *Chief Student Achievement Officer,*
Assistant Deputy Minister, Student Achievement Division,
Ontario Ministry of Education

Deep Learning captures the essence of what is pure joy for me as a learner and a leader in education. Our journey as part of the DL collaboration reenergized our teachers, students, and community to really enable students to thrive academically and socially. The collaborative inquiry cycle has brought the passion back into leading and learning by encouraging curiosity and ways to test our theories and strengthen our practices.

Teresa Stone, *Principal, Derrimut PS, Victoria, Australia,*
Leadership Advisor, Bastow Institute for Leadership, DET

DEEP LEARNING

To our cofounder Greg Butler,

Would you look at us now!

DEEP LEARNING

Engage the World Change the World

MICHAEL FULLAN
JOANNE QUINN
JOANNE McEACHEN

A JOINT PUBLICATION

FOR INFORMATION:

Corwin
A SAGE Company
2455 Teller Road
Thousand Oaks, California 91320
(800) 233-9936
www.corwin.com

SAGE Publications Ltd.
1 Oliver's Yard
55 City Road
London EC1Y 1SP
United Kingdom

SAGE Publications India Pvt. Ltd.
B 1/I 1 Mohan Cooperative Industrial Area
Mathura Road, New Delhi 110 044
India

SAGE Publications Asia-Pacific Pte. Ltd.
3 Church Street
#10-04 Samsung Hub
Singapore 049483

Publisher: Arnis Burvikovs
Development Editor: Desirée A. Bartlett
Editorial Assistants: Kaitlyn Irwin and Eliza B. Riegert
Production Editor: Melanie Birdsall
Copy Editor: Deanna Noga
Typesetter: C&M Digitals (P) Ltd.
Proofreader: Tricia Currie-Knight
Indexer: Jean Casalegno
Cover Designer: Gail Buschman
Marketing Manager: Nicole Franks

Printed in the United States of America

Library of Congress Cataloging-in-Publication Data

Names: Fullan, Michael, author. | Quinn, Joanne, author. | McEachen, Joanne, author.

Title: Deep learning : engage the world change the world / Michael Fullan, Joanne Quinn, Joanne McEachen.

Description: Thousand Oaks, California : Corwin, 2018. | Includes bibliographical references and index.

Identifiers: LCCN 2017038392 | ISBN 9781506368580 (pbk. : alk. paper)

Subjects: LCSH: Educational change. | Educational planning. | School improvement programs. | Motivation in education.

Classification: LCC LB2806 .F7933 2018 | DDC 371.2/07—dc23
LC record available at https://lccn.loc.gov/2017038392

This book is printed on acid-free paper.

SUSTAINABLE FORESTRY INITIATIVE
Certified Chain of Custody
Promoting Sustainable Forestry
www.sfiprogram.org
SFI-01268
SFI label applies to text stock

18 19 20 21 10 9 8 7 6 5 4 3 2

Contents

Chapter 1

Chapter 2

Chapter 3

Chapter 7

Chapter 8

Chapter 9

Chapter 10

Visit the companion website at
www.npdl.global
to access resources and videos.

Introduction

MAKING DEEP LEARNING A MOMENTUM MAKER

Deep learning is different in nature and scope than any other education innovation ever tried. It changes outcomes, in our case the 6Cs of global competencies: **character, citizenship, collaboration, communication, creativity,** and **critical thinking**; and it changes learning by focusing on personally and collectively meaningful matters, and by delving into them in a way that alters forever the roles of students, teachers, families, and others.

Most of all it affects the whole system—not a few individuals, or a small number of schools or districts, but *all* members of the system: children and adults alike. If one had such high aspirations—equity and excellence for the entire system—how in the world would you go about it? This is what our book is about. We can't say that we solved the problem, but we can report that we have helped unleash a torrent of new energy and corresponding insights that we try to capture in the various chapters. With our school system partners we have made substantial progress down the path of education transformation. We also know that anything new and promising can look like a shiny object for those desperately in need of a solution, or those easily led. So we worry about whether deep learning will turn out to be the siren call from Greek mythology—something appealing that lures people to go somewhere that may not end well. Nonetheless we are on the side of salvation but aware of how very demanding and counter-cultural the changes are that we write about.

On the pull side there is an explosion of technology-related learning developments underway that will only expand exponentially. We take the position that learning is the foundational driver and technology can be a great accelerator. Those who are frustrated with the current education system, including those who fight for greater equity, understandably are impatient for new results. Such restiveness can lead people to over claim. The cover of July 21, 2017, issue of the *Economist* features a picture of the brain with the caption: *The Future of Learning: How Technology Is Transforming Education*. The story is based mainly on a research study funded by the Gates Foundation, and conducted by the Rand Corporation—a report titled *Informing Progress: Insights on Personalized Learning Implementation and Effects* (Pane et al., 2017). The study was based on some 40 schools

> We take the position that learning is the foundational driver and technology can be a great accelerator.

in Next Generation Learning Challenges' (NGLC) Breakthrough School Models program. Three quarters of the schools were charter schools, and on the average were small (230 students for elementary, and 250 for high schools). All were pursuing *personalized learning* (PL) defined as "prioritizing a clear understanding of the needs and goals of each individual student and the tailoring of instruction to address those needs and goals" (Pane et al., 2017, p. 2). These PL schools were compared to a national sample of what the authors refer to as representing "more typical practice" in "traditional district schools" (p. 3). There were some indicators that showed the promise of PL, but the overall results did not reveal major differences between the two sets of schools.

Noting the fact that PL is only a small part of our model of deep learning, and that the comparison involves a group of privileged "breakthrough model" schools, the results are unimpressive to say the least. In the NGLC sample:

> Schools were implementing specific PL practices to varying degrees with *none* of the schools looking as radically different from traditional schools as theory might predict. (Pane et al., 2017, p. 2, emphasis added)

And further:

> More difficult to implement aspects did not appear to differ from practices in schools nationally, such as student discussion with teachers on progress and goals, keeping up to date documentation of student strengths, weaknesses and goals, and student choice of topics and materials. (Pane et al., 2017, p. 2)

No kidding! The Rand research is fine. It is *The Economist* that so badly wants change in public schools that it is ready to will it into existence. *The Economist* gets some of the premises right. As it notes: "Together, technology and teachers can revamp schools," and "make sure education technology narrows rather than widens inequalities" (Economist, 2017). But there is no strategy or theory of action about how to do this. We saw above from the RAND research that even privileged schools, when they get the opportunity, do not go very deeply in changing practice. Our book is different. It is based on a comprehensive model of deep learning and on its actual progress in a large number of public schools in seven countries. It is the case that good technology can accelerate good learning. In developing countries, new inexpensive adaptive software can be especially powerful for reaching large numbers of disadvantaged learners, as we will see in our own case of Uruguay.

We have been working on system change intensely since 2003. Our modus operandi is to partner with large chunks of systems to help cause significant change together, learn from it, do the next one better, learn more, and so on. We call it informed practice chasing theory to the betterment of both. We have learned that many of the best ideas come from leading practitioners, not from research per se.

The need for change and the opportunity to take action are converging. The old system works for only a minority, and those who succeed, with better marks for example, are not all that well off either when it comes to living in increasingly complex times. What's interesting is that the new set of crises is forcing humankind to reconsider its relationship to each other and to the planet and universe. The circumstances that now face us represent a unique configuration of challenges that make it essential that we proactively change the world through learning. Put another way, what Paulo Freire, the Brazilian educator and critical philosopher, saw for peasants in the 1960s, and as essential for the betterment of all, is now coming to pass on a global scale. Freire (2000) had one basic assumption, namely that humankind's "vocation" is as a subject "who acts upon and transforms the world, and in so doing moves toward ever new possibilities of a fuller and richer life individually and collectively" (p. 32). He went on to observe that in times of transition (and we need not document that now is one of those times), humans need more than ever to be connected to the "mystery of changes" that are happening.

Deep learning then is about finding our place in a complex, indeed scary world. It is about transforming our reality through learning, both individually and with others. What is significant about the "deep learning movement" is that it is not driven by policy or by the top (government). It gets its strength from the "middle" (districts and municipalities) and from the "bottom" (students, teachers). Wise policy makers will leverage and further stimulate promising deep learning developments because they come to see the necessity and desirability of having citizens who are steeped in the global competencies.

> The new set of crises is forcing humankind to reconsider its relationship to each other, and to the planet and universe; it is essential that we proactively change the world through learning.

Our book stems from work we are actually doing in partnership with schools systems around the world. We show that the status quo is fundamentally losing ground, that we are and can specify the alternative, and that the emerging breakthroughs we document are capturing the attention and immersion of students, families, and educators in what can only be called *an intentional social movement*. As such, it has the power to transform contemporary school systems. Having said that, we worry that the movement of deep learning is fragile and may become domesticated by strong forces in the status quo, or become weakened because the work becomes too complex and hard. So keep in mind that the outcome could go either way: exciting learning that is part and parcel of transforming learners and the world they inhabit, or yet another uneventful chapter in the lives of teachers and their students. The more things change, the more they stay the same. Or is there something different about the world today? We think so, and this book is about how the world of learning might turn out in profoundly better ways than the present.

Our approach to bringing about fundamental change is to work jointly with those in the system. Thus we work with all levels of the system: local schools and communities, mid-level (districts, municipalities, networks), and top-level (governments). We are, if you will, re-culturing systems in a living laboratory of learning. In particular, we are working with some 1,200 schools in seven countries in a partnership called *New Pedagogies for Deep Learning* (NPDL) including Australia, Canada, Finland, the Netherlands, New Zealand, the United States, and Uruguay (see the Appendix for a brief commentary on each country). We use the term *re-culturing* deliberately. Edgar Schein (2010)—a pioneer in the study of organizational culture—defines it as "a pattern of shared basic assumptions learned by a group as it solved its problems of external adaptation and internal integration" (p. 18). Deep learning represents a change in culture; it is not a change in program. Programs don't scale; culture does (Scott, 2017).

Programs don't scale; culture does.

We can't say that deep learning system change has occurred at scale in these cases, but there is a growing critical mass deeply engaged in the effort—enough to give us confidence that whole system change is a distinct possibility. Beyond this the good news is that there are many other examples of deep learning occurring in individual schools around the world that could be leveraged for bigger change.

We would be the first to say that the barriers are enormous: bad policies, wrong testing regimes, growing inequity that those in power try to preserve and indeed increase, inadequate and uneven investment in public education, and the complexity of proving that new deep learning is on the right track and will produce outcomes in a reasonably short time period.

We know that the uptake of deep learning on the part of students, teachers, families, and others is impressive and in some cases magnificent, as we portray and document. What we don't know is where this is heading. We can say with confidence that the current education system doesn't work and one way or the other will transform or disappear over the next two decades. Increasingly, students will not tolerate boring or alienating schooling. And the dynamics of a digitally laced global world will force radical changes whether we like it or not.

Our approach in this book is to capture what is happening in the seven countries in which we work on the deep learning agenda. It is important to understand what is already happening because in many ways it is coming from people inside the existing system. We highlight practices that are leading transformation in schools, districts, and systems. We invite you to visit **www.npdl.global** to see who we are, what we do, and why we do it. In addition to our expansive website, you will find a page of resources dedicated to this book, including the videos referenced in the chapters. To access the book's online resources, click on the *Deep Learning* book cover featured on the NPDL home page. Go to **www.npdl.global** whenever you see the online resources icon in the margins of the book.

This book is divided into three sections:

Section I: Engage the World Change the World sets the stage for powerful whole system change in learning by painting the picture of "Why deep learning?" "What makes it deep?" and "Why it matters." We then introduce a model for leading the transformation of learning in schools, districts, and systems.

Section II: The Living Laboratory examines an exciting social movement that is impacting thousands of students, teachers, and families across the globe. We use our NPDL partnership to bring definition to the concept of deep learning; identify the elements that foster the design of deep learning; explore a collaborative inquiry process that propels rapid shifts in learning and teaching practice; consider cases and vignettes illustrating the conditions and leadership that mobilize deep learning and support it to flourish at local, intermediate, and system, state, and country levels; and examine the new measures needed to assess and communicate progress in deep learning.

Section III: A Precarious Future highlights the emergent discoveries we are uncovering on the deep learning journey, identifies coherence making outcomes, and takes up the matter of how and if transformation might be possible.

Deep learning is valuable learning that *sticks*. Following Freire (2000)—and this is the central breakthrough of this book—it situates the learner as someone who acts upon the world (usually with others), thereby transforming her- or himself *and* the world itself. *Engage the world change the world* is fundamentally a learning proposition. It excites students; it excites teachers and parents; and it is the future. It is our book.

One final advance organizer concerns the question of "transformation of learning for all students" as it plays out in the course of addressing both "excellence and equity." In the course of this work, we discovered what we now call "the equity hypothesis" (Fullan & Gallagher, 2017), namely, that deep learning is good for all, but it is especially powerful for those most alienated from the traditional schooling system. Resolving the equity-excellence miasma is at the heart of societal survival, and deep learning has a starring role to play. Deep learning, as we portray it, is capable of bringing together excellence and equity for all, thereby reversing the deadly trend of growing inequality in the world. This is not just a moral question; it is a matter of survival, and even better, prosperity.

> Resolving the equity-excellence miasma is at the heart of societal survival, and deep learning is capable of bringing together excellence and equity for all, thereby reversing the deadly trend of growing inequality in the world. This is not just a moral question; it is a matter of survival, and even better, prosperity.

SECTION I
Engage the World
Change the World

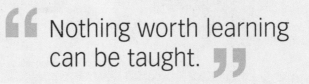

"Nothing worth learning
can be taught."

—OSCAR WILDE

Chapter 1

THE NEED FOR AND ATTRACTION OF DEEP LEARNING

Relevance Unfound

Big change is always a function of push and pull with the latter being the more powerful of the two forces. Perhaps the greatest internal push factor in traditional schooling is that it is not engaging to say the least. Lee Jenkins (2013) is one of many researchers who has examined the percentage of students who are engaged in their classrooms from kindergarten to Grade 12. He, like others, found that in kindergarten and the early grades about 95% of students are engaged followed by an ever-increasing decline to about 39% by the time students reach Grade 11. Other studies, whether from the perspective of the student or teacher, report similar declines. It has also been found that many of those who are participating are often in it for the grades, not out of interest. Gallup Poll (2016) reported that at least a third of students are "actively disengaged" and that students in Grade 11, for example, are substantially less connected to learning than Grade 5 students. All this is not so much a criticism as it is a confirmation that schooling as it was set up 150 years ago is no longer suited for the present times.

Another push factor making schooling seem less relevant is that the future job market is not only unpredictable but also in decline as the rise of robots takes its toll on the number of jobs that will be available. Compared to many of us who went through school to ensure a good future—not itself an intrinsic motivator, but it would do—the current generation has a hard time imagining the pathway to a desirable future. All this is further reinforced for students from poverty or minorities who feel a growing sense of hopelessness, because they find little sense of belonging in an institution that seems both irrelevant and uncaring.

We can draw a blunt conclusion. There is no reason for the majority of students to take conventional schooling seriously. There are many roadside attractions and other diversions that provide an alternative draw for students: drugs, the digital world, doing nothing. The easiest pathways are the ones of least resistance and instant relief, if not gratification. One of our favorite change concepts is *freedom from* versus *freedom to* (Fullan, 2015). Humans work hard to get away from something that is oppressive whether it be constraints or boredom. But they are less good at deciding what to do with any newfound freedom. In fact, the evidence is that they are vulnerable to getting into the wrong endeavor or crowd. Eric Fromm (1941, 1969), the renowned social psychologist and psychoanalyst, argued that humans find pure freedom uncomfortable and lonely, therefore are prone "either to escape from the burden of freedom into new dependencies and submission, or to advance to the full realization of positive freedom" (p. x). Apparently, advancing to realization is not so easy. So the tendency in a vacuum is to stay isolated and deteriorate or to join the wrong group. Under these conditions it takes an especially powerful pull to draw people to worthwhile endeavors. Shortly, we make the case that deep learning is such a force.

> There is no reason for the majority of students to take conventional schooling seriously.

But there are other things to worry about, and they are getting worse. There is conflict in the world. It is probably not greater than at other times in history, but it is more instantly visible and reactions are more lethal and scary in our globally connected world. We say that the big picture (where is the big world going?) and the small picture (where do I fit in?) are fusing. They are now on the same page. Even 8-year-olds and younger feel the anxiety on a daily basis. These days, because the world is so volatile and transparent, anxiety starts earlier for more kids, is prolonged for increasing numbers, and as such literally damages the brain. At the same time, access to information is exploding and immediate. Sometimes, none of the alternatives make sense: escape ostrich-like has little attraction, and knowing how to fight back or even what to fight remains mysterious. Our book is meant to help those who are willing to undertake the journey into a promising, but in many ways unknown territory. In such cases, being a good learner is the ultimate freedom.

Finally, there is another rapidly growing destructive trend, namely greater inequality in cities. Richard Florida (2017) documents, in careful detail, trends in the United States that place greater numbers of the poor "trapped in persistent poverty. . . . By 2014, 14 million Americans lived in concentrated poverty in extremely poor neighborhoods—the highest figure ever recorded and twice as many as in 2000" (p. 98).

In the course of this book, we explore the role that deep learning might play in helping reverse the deadening effects of persistent poverty, and in the last chapter we link deep learning to other policy solutions. The basic point is that from a societal perspective, and from a human vantage point, the conditions are absolutely right for a powerful, positive, compelling solution. That solution, ready to be made, is deep learning. Why do we say so, and what is deep learning in this context?

The Allure of Deep Learning

We describe here the essence of deep learning with the details of our model, along with plenty of examples, taken up in Chapter 2. What gives humans meaning in life is a strong sense of *identity* around a purpose or passion, *creativity and mastery* in relation to a valued pursuit, and *connectedness* with the world and others (for a similar list, see Mehta & Fine, 2015). The key question is not only how does one obtain this triple fulfillment, but also how do scores of people do so, especially those around us? One piece of good news is that it is easier for many people to accomplish this than it is for one of us at a time to do so, due to the power of contagion and mutual help. When we began the deep learning journey in 2014, we thought it was a compelling idea, but we did not even pose the question "Does everyone have the potential to find purpose, skill, and connection?" In implementing deep learning in scores of settings, we began to see that under the right conditions immersive learning reaches everyone. It was this realization that led us to the "equity hypothesis" referred to above: *Deep learning is good for all but is especially effective for those most disconnected from schooling.*

> Deep learning is good for all but is especially effective for those most disconnected from schooling.

To illustrate (more examples to come in subsequent chapters), let's take three examples from our work: one, a male elementary student who was disconnected from school; two, a female student who was part of a group that decided to study sustainability in Sweden; and three, a male student who found school unchallenging until the learning became relevant. All three cases are reported by the students' teachers.

Disconnected Student

Alex, Elementary Student; Ontario, Canada

This experience is shared from the perspective of a Grade One male student, Alex. Alex came to school in September with great anxiety and low self-esteem due to seeing himself as being different from everyone else because he stutters. He would rarely participate or join group tasks because of his fear of stuttering and how he would be perceived by his peers. He seemed convinced no one would want to listen to him, and he was definitely not willing to take the risk.

Early in October, our class began collaborating with a group of high school students with a diverse set of needs. Since we were not located near the high school, most of the collaboration occurred using Google Apps for Education including Google Hangouts, Google Docs, and Google Slides. As Alex became familiar with leveraging technology and as collaboration grew, so did he. I think he became so engaged in the deep learning process—solving real-world problems with his team, having the opportunity to contribute to his

(Continued)

(Continued)

own learning through research, and sharing out his ideas in new ways, as well as having his ideas validated by not only his peers but also high school students—that the risk-taking and speaking just naturally evolved as part of the process. It was beautiful to watch! And that was Grade One.

The following year in Grade Two, Alex spoke before our school Board of Trustees to discuss his learning experiences. Here is a quote from his speech:

> I still remember when I didn't talk that much. I never would have thought I could be a public speaker!! So how did this happen? Grade One, that's how.

He went on to share even more about deep learning:

> I was excited with the learning that was happening in my class. I had choice in my learning. I got to learn with technology and that's the way my brain works. Most importantly for me, collaboration was expected and happened every day. Collaboration is important to me because my ideas get bigger when I share with other people and then my brain gets bigger.

Now, Alex is in Grade Three, and there is no stopping him! Our school gathered as a community of learners to celebrate math and share best practices with parents. Alex was leading the Math Talk portion of the workshops. He was encouraging parents to collaborate, to participate and validating the ideas of everyone. If I had not been there that September morning to witness this child previously so full of anxiety, so fearful to speak and unable to take risks, I would never believe it could possibly be the same student I now know today.

6Cs Go to Sweden

Mara, Middle School Student; Ottawa, Canada

Mara is in a middle school that calls itself a "6Cs school" (6Cs: character, citizenship, collaboration, communication, creativity, and critical thinking). As part of a school initiative, a group of 13-year-old students with their principal and teachers planned to visit and study sustainability in Sweden. The following is an excerpt from Mara, a student who very creatively submitted a suitcase filled with travel documents including a boarding pass and a list of things to remember as her application for one of 12 spots on the trip. She also included her narrative, which speaks of the importance of the 6Cs:

> What some people may not know is that the 6Cs aren't just words and posters around the school. They are part of our lifestyle

whether we realize it or not. To some people those words (the 6Cs) may not mean anything special but at [our school] it is a highly incorporated part of our school life and our community. I know that I use the 6Cs at home with my family and when I interact with the world around me.

Some things I hope to accomplish is to compare school life between our school and the Swedish school, create memories with school mates and teachers, take back helpful tips to improve our community based on what I've learned, and perhaps introduce the 6Cs to my Swedish housemate.

Disengaged Student

Christopher, Student; Ontario, Canada

At the beginning of the school year, Christopher was unenthused, and it seemed like he was counting down the time to recess, lunch, and finally, dismissal. He was one of the kids on my radar, and I was starting to get worried that his mindset would start to have an effect on his academic progress in his Grade Four year.

In our French Immersion class this year, we started off with a simple question that a student shared: "Can kids make a difference in the world?" As a teacher, little did I know how far this question would end up taking us on a yearlong deep learning journey that embedded traits of social entrepreneurialism and citizenship. When we started talking about how to enact change and truly make a difference in one's life, Christopher was absolutely beaming. His hand was always firing up, and his ideas were truly innovative. There was no stopping him, really, and his passion extended far beyond the four walls of the classroom.

With the help of a business partner from The Bank of Montreal, students were tasked with creating their own business with the goal of selling either a product or a service to a target market in the community. When students were tasked with coming up with ideas on what to do, it was Christopher who took on a leadership role and started positively collaborating with students in the classroom to brainstorm the perfect idea that would sell so that we could make lots of money for cancer research. We ended up having a Dragon's Den to persuasively pitch our products and services to the class, and it was Christopher's group that won the pitch! Their idea was to design and sell customized silicone bracelets to our school community.

Beyond our business, we came across and nurtured many different learning partnerships that continue to inspire students to this day. Without Christopher, many of these partnerships may not have been uprooted. It

(Continued)

(Continued)

was Christopher who mentioned that we should know more about where our every dollar is going regarding cancer research, and with that idea, students decided that they wanted to have a Google Hangout with The Terry Fox Foundation (the cancer foundation we were supporting) to get answers to some of their questions.

It was Christopher's high energy and enthusiasm that kept this venture running from October 2016 to June of 2017. There was not one day after we started this journey that he wouldn't ask to stay in during recess to work on anything related to the project (marketing, communications, awareness, finances, etc.). His heart and spirit were truly vested in the work we were doing. His attitude toward school changed, and his eagerness to continue making change in the world inspired even more students in the school to create their own business to support a worthwhile cause.

I can wholeheartedly say that this venture opened up Christopher's eyes in ways that were unimaginable to me from the start of the year. So many of the global competencies were uprooted through Christopher's work, and as an educator, his zest for real-world change inspired me to allow students to take the helm with their learning and pave their own pathways. When the students have a voice, it can drive any project you work on in directions that were unimaginable from the start.

Of course, one could always find individual students, such as those just mentioned, in this or that school working with outstanding teachers, but our book is about scores of students in systems of schools whereby leaders at schools, districts, municipalities, and even whole countries decide to implement deep learning across the system. Is it possible for virtually all students to flourish though deep learning? From our work with thousands of students and educators, we think that it is not only possible but also essential to the future of the world.

Most often when students or groups of students persistently show no interest in learning, we write them off as incapable or unteachable. We might give them remedial work that ends up adding insult to injury where boredom becomes tedium or other forms of punishment where the distance to connection becomes even greater. Our work is beginning to prove that *every child is a hidden figure* (a metaphor based on the movie of the same name where a group of behind-the-scenes black women with special math abilities played a critical part in saving a NASA space mission and building the space agency's successful future).

Students alienated from present society are the most distant from learning, but all students in today's world need to figure out where they fit in a complex global society. Many of these children and teenagers are truly hidden as street kids, foster children, and otherwise outside of mainstream society. Beyond this, each and every student, no matter how advantaged, will at some point find herself or himself at sea in today's turmoil. Every individual to some extent is a mystery to herself or himself, to each other, and to the universe. The role of education is to help individuals come out of their private shells or personal hells in ways that address obstacles.

Preliminary data show that the trajectory of alienation for poor and rich kids alike could be very different. Put a young person in a stagnant situation or one demanding irrelevant activities, and they will appear unreachable. But put them in a deep learning environment, and these same young people will be ready to change the world. We know because we have seen it time and time again.

Deep Learning:

- Increases self and others' expectations for more learning and achievement by providing a process

- Increases student engagement in the learning through personalization and ownership

- Connects students to the "real world," which is often more reflective of their own reality and cultural identity, which can be particularly important for students from other cultures

- Resonates with spiritual values that link to vast numbers of the population whether secular or religious

- Builds skills, knowledge, self-confidence, and self-efficacy through inquiry

- Builds new relationships with and between the learner, their family, their communities, and their teachers

- Deepens human desire to connect with others to do good

The Challenge

The challenge is enormous, but we offer a way forward, which is essentially: *go deep or go home.* And *be pervasive (system minded) or stand aside.* It will be incredibly difficult to make system headway, but we can only say that a number of ingredients for system success are emerging, and that given the growing crises in the world, there is no other viable game in town. It is for these and other reasons that deep learning is taking hold in New Pedagogies for Deep Learning schools. Once educators, students, and their families experience the excitement and learning potential of deep learning, they become more committed, and as they interact with others, the contagion factor sets in. Over 3 years we have seen a growing uptake from

Once educators, students, and their families experience the excitement and learning potential of deep learning, they become more committed, and as they interact with others, the contagion factor sets in.

500 to 1,200 schools in seven countries. Uruguay went from 100 to 400 schools, Finland from 100 to over 200, and three large districts in Ontario went from 10% to 100% of their schools. In other cases, some districts or groups did not expand as rapidly. Thus, we are not saying that deep learning represents an automatic pathway to transformation. There are many forces that reinforce the status quo and that rein in innovations once they get started. But at the end of the day, our experience is that deep learning is a natural momentum maker if the key pieces are put in place and cultivated.

If all children can learn, can all teachers learn? Are the incredible and rapid developments in the neuroscience of learning a game changer for us all, including those most damaged? Was Paulo Freire (1974) right in concluding that humankind's ultimate vocation in times of transition is to engage the world to change the world (this as noted is a fundamental deep learning proposition)? Can partnering with young people from babies onward unleash the masses we need to upend the status quo, since young people not only have no allegiance to the status quo, but also positively can be impassioned to "help humanity"?

The goal is to make deep learning a momentum maker. In social movements, people are attracted to *new ideas* that embody treasured values and promise new *outcomes and impact*. It is the ideas more than particular leaders that mobilize people. Make deep learning the positive pull factor of the decade—people are ready for it, even if they don't know so until they experience it.

In the next two chapters, we establish some of the basics of deep learning in action.

Make deep learning the positive pull factor of the decade—people are ready for it, even if they don't know so until they experience it.

Notes

" Any fool can know. The point is to understand. "

—OFTEN ATTRIBUTED
TO ALBERT EINSTEIN

Chapter 2

WHAT'S DEEP ABOUT DEEP LEARNING?

Reimagining Learning

If we want learners who can thrive in turbulent, complex times, apply thinking to new situations, and change the world, we must reimagine learning: what's important to be learned, how learning is fostered, where learning happens, and how we measure success. This means creating environments that challenge, provoke, stimulate, and celebrate learning. We call this new conceptualization of the learning process **deep learning,** and it must become the new purpose of education.

We have asked ourselves what would an environment that truly causes students to flourish look like, and feel like. Recently, Daan Roosegaarde, a Dutch designer, architect, and innovator, shared some provocative suggestions for reimagining the learning process in a keynote address (NPDL Global Deep Learning Lab, May 1, 2017, Toronto). He describes himself as a reformer who wants to create interactive sustainable environments that are at once functional and beautiful looking, to make the world better for humankind. He always begins with "why." For example, he began wondering why we spend so much on cars and leave our road design in the middle ages. This led him to create paints that charge with solar energy in the daytime and give light at night. Next, Roosegaarde took that technology to the Vincent Van Gogh Museum, which is set back in a large park. To make visiting more interactive, he created a bike path made of bricks that use solar power gathered during the day to light the magical pathway and guide riders through the dark. Later on a visit to China, Roosegaarde was struck by how the view from his hotel on the first day was completely veiled by smog obscuring everything on the second day. So he set out to create the largest vacuum cleaner in the world that would suck up pollution from the sky and clean it by removing particles of carbon. The result was the creation of parks that were 55% to 75% cleaner than the rest of the city. Roosegaarde's team then compressed the carbon and created smog-free rings that contribute clean air to the city; and the team is now working on bicycles that will do the same. He readily admits this is a partial solution (we also need to reduce the emissions themselves), but it illustrates

> If we want learners who can thrive in turbulent, complex times, apply thinking to new situations, and change the world, we must reimagine learning.

what happens when we ask the right questions and remove barriers to new thinking (see more examples at www.studioroosegaarde.net).

Roosegaarde is forthright in stating that he did not fit into the normal schooling, but once he began to follow his innate curiosity, his talent and passion were unleashed. He suggests to educators that we cultivate rich learning environments for children.

Roosegaarde's Suggestions for How to Cultivate Learning Environments for Children

1. Create learning driven by *curiosity* where "learners are infiltrators and shapers of the future." This means working on real issues of relevance to themselves and the world.

2. Teach students to be *problem designers*. This shifts the starting point from thinking in terms of opinions of "what is" to thinking of proposals of "what could be."

3. Pose problems in which children can be *involved,* not just asked to solve. Provide opportunities for finding solutions to new ambiguities, not just finding an answer to a problem that already has been answered.

4. Foster living as a *perpetual amateur* where learning is all about taking risks and is a lifelong venture.

5. Believe children will *exceed all our expectations*—where we teach them not to be scared (of the unknown) but rather to be curious.

6. Recognize that innovation and creativity are already in the DNA of every human being.

Finally, Roosegaarde observes that our quest is *not about re-inventing the bike but about finding new ways to ride the bike.* We don't have to create the learning process but rather find ways to redefine it so we unleash this natural potential for learning. The good news is that children are innately curious, so we just need to challenge them. We need to have a "launch and learn mentality" where discoveries are cherished and then refined, not marked right or wrong. We need places of learning that celebrate and appreciate that not everyone is the same or follows the same learning journey. We need to create places that foster persistence and passion, and where a mistake is only a mistake if you don't learn from it. We need to design environments that help learners dream and then challenge them to take action.

In 2014, we took up the challenge of how to create deep learning so that *all* students can flourish in a complex world. We founded a global partnership, New Pedagogies for Deep Learning (NPDL), with more than 1,200 schools in seven countries. This living laboratory is committed to identifying the practices and conditions that will transform the process of learning so that every student develops the essential skills and global competencies. Early evidence is emerging of students becoming agents of change in influencing their own learning while acting as catalysts of societal change. This shift in pedagogy is transforming the roles of all learning partners—students, educators, and families alike.

So let's take a look at what's happening in classrooms, schools, and systems that are part of this social movement. Stop by a deep learning classroom and you will see students who are voraciously curious and who are encouraged to ask questions of each other, teachers, families, and experts across the community or globe. There's a constant buzz of conversation as students grapple with solving problems or investigating ideas so they can make sense of their world. Everyone is highly focused, and as a visitor you may not be noticed, but if you listen in you will find students able to articulate what they are doing and why. They are able to describe the skills they are mastering and the ways they will need to get better. They lose track of time because the task is engaging and often work at home and on weekends because their imagination and interest have been captured. They take pride in describing their work for classmates or community members because it is meaningful, authentic, and relevant—it makes a difference.

In schools where deep learning is taking root, we see similar behaviors in the adults. Wander from classroom to classroom and you will see teachers moving about, interacting with individuals and small groups, asking questions, facilitating access to resources, and giving timely feedback. Teachers are collaborating with each other on the design of learning as well as to assess growth. There is a pervasive transparency of practice, common language, and shared expectations across these schools. Meetings usually focus on how well the students are learning and how to use the tools and processes to accelerate or amplify learning rather than to discuss *problem* students. School leaders are frequently in classrooms and in discussions with groups of teachers on how to make the learning better. Logistical and administrative issues don't disappear but are more often handled by digital and other processes so that precious face-to-face time is freed up for learning. Parents are welcomed as partners in these schools, where they play an active role, and meetings with parents focus more on sharing evidence of student progress and learning.

Finally, where deep learning is accelerating, we see the system playing a vital role. While classrooms and schools can innovate and create havens of deep learning on their own, they are fragile. People come and go, the inspired leadership leaves, and the status quo creeps back in. In contrast, where we see the greatest acceleration, there is a strategic role played by the system, which may be a municipality, a district, a cluster, or a network. Visit a number of schools in any one of these groupings and you come away with a sense of a common language and set of expectations. There is agreement emerging from continual dialogue of what deep learning is and how to get more of it. Teachers and leaders are transparent in their practice and share expertise, tools, and resources. The work is celebrated, and accountability resides in getting and sharing evidence of student learning, not obsessing about external testing.

We are seeing glimpses of this new kind of learning across the globe. It combines a repositioning of learning relationships among students, families, educators, policy makers, and society as a whole with focusing on a new set of outcomes. So why is this energizing, engaging learning not taking root spontaneously in all classrooms, schools, and systems? While these examples give us a feel for new ways of learning, we must be more deliberate about spreading it. And if we want deep learning to flourish and be accessible to all, we need to be more precise about what we mean by *deep learning*.

Where deep learning is accelerating, we see the system playing a vital role.

What Is Deep Learning?

The NPDL partner countries took into account the changing global dynamic, connectivity, and societal changes. They recognized that at the same time that students are facing a more challenging world, the days of set knowledge and accomplishment based on content are over. Put another way, Andreas Schleicher, director of education and skills of Organisation for Economic Co-operation and Development (OECD, 2016), suggests that this creates a new dynamic for graduates who will not be paid for what they know but rather for what they can do. This movement away from set knowledge to the skills of entrepreneurship, creativity, and problem solving suggests a new set of competencies necessary to thrive in this accelerating world.

Teachers, leaders, and policy makers spent long hours discussing and debating what was essential and distinctive for students to know, be able to do, and most important, be like as human citizens. The result of our work is the identification of six global competencies that describe the skills and attributes needed for learners to flourish as citizens of the world. In our definition, *deep learning is the process of acquiring these six global competencies: character, citizenship, collaboration, communication, creativity, and critical thinking.* These competencies encompass compassion, empathy, socio-emotional learning, entrepreneurialism, and related skills required for high functioning in a complex universe.

Deep Learning is the process of acquiring these six global competencies: character, citizenship, collaboration, communication, creativity, and critical thinking.

Simply naming the six competencies was a step toward clarity but did not help educators, students, or families have a *shared* depth of understanding of what they meant. Each of the six has several dimensions. Our goal is to bring clarity to a set of concepts that are often recognized vaguely across educators. For example, critical thinking is probably the most readily recognized, yet ask 10 teachers what it means to be a critical thinker and you will get diverse answers. Then ask how they will measure the depth of that critical thinking, and the response becomes even fuzzier. So we developed a set of definitions for each competency, as shown in Figure 2.1.

Figure 2.1 • Defining the Six Global Competencies for Deep Learning

	Character • Learning to learn • Grit, tenacity, perseverance, and resilience • Self-regulation, responsibility, and integrity
	Citizenship • Thinking like global citizens • Considering global issues based on a deep understanding of diverse values and worldviews • Genuine interest and ability to solve ambiguous and complex real-world problems that impact human and environmental sustainability • Compassion, empathy, and concern for others
	Collaboration • Working interdependently and synergistically in teams • Interpersonal and team-related skills • Social, emotional, and intercultural skills • Managing team dynamics and challenges • Learning from and contributing to the learning of others
	Communication • Communicating effectively with a variety of styles, modes, and tools including digital • Communication designed for different audiences • Reflection on and use of the process of learning to improve communication
	Creativity • Having an "entrepreneurial eye" for economic and social opportunities • Asking the right inquiry questions • Considering and pursuing novel ideas and solutions • Leadership to turn ideas into action
	Critical Thinking • Evaluating information and arguments • Making connections and identifying patterns • Problem solving • Constructing meaningful knowledge • Experimenting, reflecting, and taking action on ideas in the real world

Source: Copyright © 2014 by New Pedagogies for Deep Learning™ (NPDL)

This greater specificity led to the beginning of a common language about what the competencies would look like in practice. Teachers, students, families, and leaders began to share their thinking and perspectives. We discovered that while precise definitions helped guide discussion, they were still not sufficient for us to measure growth on the competencies or to help differentiate learning tasks. This led us to develop a new way of defining the pathway for developing each competency and measuring progress. We called these *learning progressions*.

Some ask why use the term *competencies* when the language of skills and abilities is more common and understood? We use the term *competency* to denote a set of multilayered capacities that combine knowledge, skills, and attitudes about self and others. The use of *competencies* was reinforced in a recent OECD paper, *Global Competence in an Inclusive World* (2016), where the case is made that:

> Global Competence includes the acquisition of in-depth knowledge and understanding of global and intercultural issues; the ability to learn from and live with people from diverse backgrounds; and the attitudes and values necessary to interact respectfully with others. (p. 1)

At first glance, our list of competencies may appear similar to others for 21st century learning (*collaboration, critical thinking, communication,* and *creativity* make most lists), but simply naming the competencies has little impact by itself. Educators, networks, and commissions have been describing 21st century skills for at least 20 years with little robust implementation or effective ways to assess them. Moreover, there has been little focus on the *how*, few large-scale attempts at implementation, and little evidence of significant concrete change in learning and teaching practices.

Our global competencies, or the 6Cs as we often refer to them, differ from other 21st century lists in three crucial ways: comprehensiveness, precision, and measurability.

Unique Characteristics of the Global Competencies (6Cs)

Comprehensiveness: In addition to communication, collaboration, creativity, and critical thinking, we added character and citizenship. These two competencies are proving to be game changers that allow students to focus on complex problems, take responsibility for their learning, and have concern for and contribute to the world. Think back to the earlier examples where students are drawing on all 6Cs—simultaneously focusing their work on helping humanity locally and globally, building their character skills of grit and perseverance, and leading their own learning.

Deep learning occurs when we use the competencies to engage in issues and tasks of value to students and the world.

Character and citizenship are foundational qualities that bring to life the skills and behaviors of creativity, collaboration, critical thinking, and communication. Finally, creativity—the poor cousin of the original four—has found a new catalytic life by permeating all 6Cs in action. Novel solutions to persistent problems.

Precision: Making deep learning actionable meant creating a more robust set of attributes and skills for each competency and creating ways to measure their development. For each competency a *deep learning progression* was created. Each competency is broken into five to six dimensions that provide a picture of the skills, capabilities, and attitudes needed to develop that competency. Figure 2.2 depicts a sample of the Deep Learning Progression for Collaboration. The full learning progression is found in Figure 9.1. The progressions serve as an anchor for professional dialogue in designing deep learning experiences and also as a monitoring and evaluation system during the learning process.

Measurability: The deep learning progressions are used by students and teachers to assess starting points, develop shared language about success in each competency, facilitate competency development, monitor progress, and measure learners' growth on a continuum over time.

The precision of defining the competencies and the robustness of the deep learning progressions has been crucial in two ways. First, they have provided a common language for students, teachers, and families in the design and measurement of learning. This has led to greater co-design and co-assessment of results. Second, the progressions are anchors for rich discussions that lead to greater precision and intentionality in the design, monitoring, and measurement of learning. We are working on measuring the 6Cs as outcomes of deep learning that students will take forward into their post-secondary lives.

As teachers began to use a common language and the 6Cs, they noted that these competencies are fostered most often in learning experiences that have certain characteristics (see the box on the top of page 21).

Deep learning occurs when we use the competencies to engage in issues and tasks of value to students and the world. More and more we are finding that while deep learning is essential for all, it is especially a turning point for students from disadvantaged backgrounds and those underserved by conventional schooling.

Why Deep Learning Matters

As we noted earlier, one theme in particular is emerging from the deep learning work as we see more and more students from both advantaged and challenged circumstances flourishing: *equity and excellence are feeding on each other*! We are coming to the conclusion that these two phenomena are

New Pedagogies for
Deep Learning™
A GLOBAL PARTNERSHIP

Figure 2.2 • Deep Learning Progression: Collaboration

Collaboration Deep Learning Progression

Work interdependently and synergistically in teams with strong interpersonal and team-related skills including effective management of team dynamics and challenges, making substantive decisions together, and learning from and contributing to the learning of others.

Dimension	Limited Evidence	Emerging	Developing	Accelerating	Proficient
Working interdependently as a team	Learners either work individually on learning tasks or collaborate informally in pairs or groups but do not really work together as a team. Learners may discuss some issues or content together but skip over important substantive decisions (such as how the process will be managed), which has significant adverse impacts on how well the collaboration works.	Learners work together in pairs or groups and are responsible for completing a task for the group to achieve its work. At this level, tasks may not be well matched to each individual's strengths and expertise, and group members' contributions may not be equitable. Learners are starting to make some decisions together but may still be leaving the most important substantive decisions to one or two members.	Learners decide together how to match tasks to the individual strengths and expertise of team members and then work effectively together in pairs or groups. Learners involve all members in making joint decisions about an important issue, problem, or process and developing a team solution.	Learners can articulate how they work together in a way that is interdependent and uses each person's strengths in the best possible way to make sound substantive decisions and develop ideas and solutions. Interdependent teamwork is clearly evident in that learners' contributions are woven together to communicate an overarching idea and/or create a product.	Learners demonstrate a highly effective and synergistic approach to working interdependently in a way that not only leverages each member's strengths but also provides opportunities for each to build on those strengths and learn new skills. This includes ensuring that substantive decisions are discussed at a deep level that ensures each team member's strengths and perspectives are infused to come to the best possible decision that benefits all.
Interpersonal and team-related skills	Although learners may help each other on tasks that contribute to a joint work product or outcome, interpersonal and team-related skills are not yet evident. Learners do not yet demonstrate a genuine sense of empathy or a shared purpose for working together.	Learners report and demonstrate a sense of collective ownership of the work and show some interpersonal and team-related skills. The focus is on achieving a common or joint outcome, product, design, response, or decision, but at this level the key decisions may be taken or dominated by one or two members.	Learners demonstrate not only good interpersonal skills and collective ownership of the work, but an active sense of shared responsibility is also evident. From beginning to end, the team listens effectively and negotiates and agrees on the goals, content, process, design, and conclusions of their work.	Learners can clearly articulate how joint responsibility for the work and its product or outcome pervades the entire task. Strong skills in listening, facilitation, and effective teamwork ensure that all voices are heard and reflected in the ways of working or work product.	Learners take an active responsibility, both individually and collectively, for ensuring that the collaborative process works as effectively as possible, that each person's ideas and expertise are used to maximum advantage, and that each work product or outcome is of the highest possible quality or value.

Source: McEachen, J., & Quinn, J. *Collaboration Deep Learning Progression.* Copyright © 2014 by New Pedagogies for Deep Learning™ (NPDL)

Learning Experiences That Foster the 6Cs

1. Involve higher-order cognitive processes to reach a deep understanding of content and issues in a contemporary world

2. Include immersion in addressing areas or issues that are often cross disciplinary

3. Integrate academic and personal capabilities

4. Are active, authentic, challenging, and student centered

5. Are often designed to impact the world, locally or more widely

6. Take place in a range of settings and increasingly use digital and connectivity

intertwined and that we can only achieve well-being if we attend to both equity and excellence. Some students have much further to go if they are seriously disconnected from the world, but the world is becoming so complex to navigate that the majority of all students will need help in finding their place in the world.

Well-Being

Well-being has gained worldwide attention across countries and organizations such as the OECD, who are recognizing that students need far more than academic development to thrive. Ontario's Ministry of Education defines *well-being* as "a positive sense of self, spirit, and belonging that we feel when our cognitive, emotional, social and physical needs are being met. It is supported through equity and respect for our diverse identities and strengths" (2016, p. 3). Well-being in early years and school settings is about helping children and students become resilient so that they can make positive and healthy choices to support learning and achievement both now and in the future. Ontario's approach for promoting well-being attends to four developmental domains: cognitive, physical, social, and emotional, with self and spirit at the center (see Figure 2.3).

The deep learning work and six global competencies are grounded in the fundamentals of neuroscience and address the four domains. One of Ontario's education policy advisors, Dr. Jean Clinton, a child psychiatrist, has recently

> We see more and more students from both advantaged and challenged circumstances flourishing: *equity and excellence are feeding on each other*!

CHAPTER 2

Figure 2.3 • Four Developmental Domains of Well-Being

immersed herself in our deep learning work and the examples that illustrated vulnerable students tackling problems relevant to their life circumstances. She made a startling observation that "a focus on the 6Cs immunizes and protects against social and emotional difficulties thus building positive mental health and resilience. A focus on the 6Cs levels the playing field for kids from challenging backgrounds" ("Connection Through," June, 2017).

Clinton (2013) points to the strong relational aspect to brain development. This begins in infancy when the child is picked up and soothed, because it is receiving messages of safety and belonging that change the neurons and create new neural pathways that allow the child to handle stress in later life. This builds capacity to form relationships and manage and self-regulate emotions. Children need adults and peers who can co-manage and let the child know what is inside and outside of bounds if they are to be able to manage and express emotions appropriately. When these messages are not given in the early years for any reason, it is even more important that we create classrooms that build a sense of belonging. Clinton suggests that schools represent a massive, invisible classroom where teachers, students, and others are passing constant messages that impact well-being—many of them nonverbal about belonging and connectedness.

A second aspect of brain development linked to deep learning is its remarkable capacity to grow and change throughout life. Plasticity, the ability to

"A focus on the 6Cs immunizes and protects against social and emotional difficulties thus building positive mental health and resilience. A focus on the 6Cs levels the playing field for kids from challenging backgrounds."
(Dr. Jean Clinton)

grow new neural pathways, is intense in the early years of birth to age 6 and thus responds to stimulation of all kinds, both cognitive and emotional. A second burst of massive change occurs in adolescence, where a pruning of the neural pathways increases efficiency and habits for life.

The key implication for educators is that brain development can be shaped by the social-emotional conditions as well as the cognitive stimulation from choice and authentic learning.

> My thinking is that in a classroom focusing on the 6Cs there is created a very strong sense of relationship-safety between the teacher, students, students to each other and also importantly the student to the space of learning. For example, in order to create a collaborative space and stance the teacher has to model empathy and compassion for the differences amongst the group. A focus on communication requires students and teachers to truly listen to the other and ask questions like "tell me what you meant" rather than "use your words." . . . This implies a belief in the competency and capabilities of every child and a belief that every child *can* learn. (Clinton, 2017, personal communication)

We must attend to language, thinking, and emotions simultaneously because children learn best in an environment that acknowledges the inter-connectivity of both cognitive and emotional development. This has even more impact on achieving equity for children who arrive at school without benefit of this connectedness and stimulation.

The Equity Hypothesis

Some students arrive on the doorsteps of schools every day without readiness to learn. This disadvantage may stem from living in intergenerational poverty, living with the terror of being a refugee, homelessness, neglect, or lack of stimulation. Equity has been a focus of policy makers for decades, but it often addresses only issues of access and uses remedial programs "to catch up," a dumbing down of expectations, and pull-out programs that further alienate and disengage students from peers.

We know, for example, that children of poverty may arrive in kindergarten with 300 words versus other more privileged children who have 1,200 or more words they know and use. Not only are they limited in communication, but they also may not recognize the requests being made of them—"please put your backpack inside your cubbyhole" could be ignored because they don't know what a backpack is or what a cubbyhole means. The stance and mindset of the teachers is crucial: Do they connect or correct? Do they see this as an opportunity to build communication or interpret it as defiance or apathy? We believe teachers who build relationships around belonging, purpose, and hope can then leverage those relationships through the lens of the 6Cs to bring the cognitive to life (see Chapters 5 and 6).

In our deep learning work, the "old" notion that students who have struggled with school must wait until they have mastered the foundations of literacy and numeracy are being replaced with effective programs that bolster foundational literacy and numeracy skills but simultaneously engross students in authentic tasks that engage them deeply while providing meaningful ways to learn critical literacy skills. We call this the *equity hypothesis*, noting emerging evidence that suggests deep learning is necessary for all but may be even more advantageous for those alienated and underserved by traditional schools. Indeed, there is a strong case to be made that we need to tackle *inequity with excellence*—defined as deep learning (doing something in depth that has personal and collective meaning). The tweet would be "Don't dumb down; smarten up!"

In short, deep learning, positioned to engage the disconnected, could turn out to be a force for reversing the damaging effects of concentrated, intergenerational poverty and racism. Noguera, Darling-Hammond, and Friedlaender (2015) reported that schools that engaged low-income and minority students in deep learning "have stronger academic outcomes, better attendance and student behavior, lower dropout rates, . . . and higher rates of college attendance and perseverance than comparison schools serving similar students" (p. 8). Similar results in a study by the American Institute for Research (AIR, 2014) of teacher practices, support structures, and student outcomes in 19 high schools suggest that students in schools pursuing a deep learning agenda fare better. They were more likely to finish high school, go to college, get higher scores on achievement tests, do better on assessments of problem solving, and rate themselves higher on measures of engagement, motivation, and self-efficacy (Heller & Wolfe, 2015; Huberman, Bitter, Anthony, & O'Day, 2014; Zeisr, Taylor, Rickles, Garet, & Segeritz, 2014). The problem in these cases is that up to this point successes occur on a very small scale; they are exceptions to the norm. Our quest is to make deep learning a characteristic of the entire system.

Anti-prejudice policies are essential but not sufficient to address our equity and excellence hypothesis. There must be strategies that enable all students to thrive as learners in addition to directly eradicating prejudice and proactively teaching the value of diversity in society. Reducing the injustice does not in itself increase well-being or outcomes. As an Ontario First Nations leader stated: "In our culture we believe that every child is born with gifts. . . . What will our schools do to uncover and develop the gifts of our children?" (as quoted in Ontario Ministry of Education, 2014a). Deep learning focuses on equipping all students with the six global competencies that will allow them to thrive while creating the conditions for learning. We believe that the pathway to well-being is through deep learning experiences that address equity and excellence, and we highlight numerous examples in the coming chapters.

It's All About Re-Culturing

Deep learning experiences are erupting across our NPDL world and spreading. Interest in deep learning is also accelerating among policy makers and practitioners from countries, states, provinces, districts, and schools. More and more educators are saying to us, "We agree deep learning is needed, but *how* do we do it on a large scale?" The challenge is not simply "How do we cause this to happen in a single classroom or school?" We see innovative teachers and schools on Twitter and social media sites daily. The challenge is *how* do we do this for *all* classrooms in a school, all schools in a district or municipality, and a whole state, province, or country? Individuals can buck the system; groups are needed to upend it.

So where should education begin if one wants a different outcome? This is really a chicken or egg dilemma. Some proponents for change argue that schools are obsolete and therefore we must dismantle the current system to allow students to design their own learning, free of all constraints. There is an underlying theory of change in this scenario that *if only* we had no buildings, no districts, no content disciplines, and no measurements, *then* students would be free to learn deeply. An increasingly diverse and available digital world does make such learning possible, but there is no reason to believe that all students would avail themselves of the opportunity, or that the outcome would address systemic inequality.

The polar opposite of the "dismantle the system" position is to continue tinkering and making incremental improvements—the latest being new learning standards and measures. This is playing out in the United States with the introduction of the Common Core State Standards (CCSS)—which itself has a number of problems—and the federal passage of the Every Student Succeeds Act (ESSA). The theory of change in these endeavors suggests that new descriptions of learning outcomes and measurements will somehow create new skills in teachers and unleash student potential and engagement. While these two policies are a step toward potential change, they fall short of providing a mechanism for growth. The problem is that describing and measuring outcomes—the "what"—does little to change the skill and knowledge of teachers and leaders to foster new forms of learning, which could lead to the new outcomes. What is missing in current approaches is a robust strategy to get at the "how" of improvement.

So what needs to happen first? Do we begin with changing all the structures and rules or tinker with the status quo? Focusing on structural change can be a distracter and time consumer. It is impractical to think that eliminating school buildings and the role of teachers and replacing it with student-led learning could happen at scale rapidly. Any superintendent who has ever needed to close a school due to declining enrollment can attest to the emotional and even irrational resistance communities express when they feel that something (even an out-of-date building) is being taken away. Changes to buildings, university admissions, teacher preparation, curriculum, technology, time, and measurements would all contribute to facilitating deep learning, but waiting for them to change as a precondition for moving forward is futile. If systems focus efforts on structural changes only, they will have no greater expertise in fostering deep learning experiences. On the flip side, tinkering with the status quo addresses parts of the system, but rarely considers the whole. As a result, improvements are fragmented and never add up to whole system change.

We propose that putting the *process of learning* at the heart of change is a much more productive approach. Mobilizing collective action to focus on the process of learning changes relationships and develops new pedagogical practices, which in turn pushes the structures to change. It is crucial to recognize that shifting to a focus on the process of learning represents a *change in culture*. The latter not only alters the relationships between and among students, teachers, and families, but also fundamentally changes the relationships among teachers and between teachers and administrators. Any change worth doing requires focused collaboration! We saw this in previous work in whole system change with districts implementing Learning Communities. Those who were preoccupied with establishing dedicated time before they had experience with meaningful collaborative work often ended up with time blocks on a schedule but little purpose, trust, or the relationships and focus necessary to impact student learning. Schools and districts that began by focusing on using any small amounts of time to collaboratively improve learning saw the benefits and then exploited the structures to create conditions for what needed to be done.

Final Thoughts

The change lesson here is that we need to change the *culture of learning*, not simply the trappings or structures. It cannot be done by policies or mandates. Transformation will only occur when we engage in the work of facilitating new processes for learning. Once we have agreed on the learning outcomes or competencies described earlier in this chapter, we need to provide rich opportunities to work collaboratively, build new learning relationships, and learn from the work. No amount of preplanning is better than the common experience of learning together while doing the work, because it builds capacity and ownership simultaneously. Simply put, *we learn more from doing than thinking about doing,* so if we want deep learning, we need to get started.

Thus, leadership for change is crucial—leadership that comes from all quarters. We now turn to our framework for leading re-culturing and the transformation of learning.

The change lesson here is that we need to change the *culture of learning,* not simply the trappings or structures.

Notes

_____

_____

_____

_____

_____

_____

_____

_____

_____

_____

_____

_____

_____

_____

_____

_____

_____

_____

_____

CHAPTER 2

" For the simplicity that lies
this side of complexity,
I would not give a fig, but for
the simplicity that lies on the
other side of complexity,
I would give my life. "

—OLIVER WENDELL HOLMES JR.

Chapter 3

LEADING TRANSFORMATION

Coherence Making for Whole System Change

As we immerse ourselves in this deep learning work, we can say three things for sure. First, the forces for deep learning have now been unleashed. Deep learning exists and will rapidly become more and more evident. The second is that *leadership* for system transformation will come from all quarters and indeed is increasingly more likely to come from students and teachers as change agents. Third, the nature of transformation will be fraught with ambiguity, accompanied by periods of setbacks, clarity, and breakthroughs even in those cases where leadership is sound. Be prepared for a journey into the unknown. The only salvation is that doing nothing means that one becomes a pawn in the inevitable change forces that are now occurring in society with greater complexity and speed.

It's time for a more powerful, deep theory of change that transforms whole systems. What's emerging is a change strategy that fosters a whole system culture of growth and innovation as it catalyzes an ecosystem of players, builds capacity, and mobilizes coherent action. In this chapter, we examine a framework for developing coherent whole system change and then will zero in on how to apply whole system change to deep learning.

We took up the challenge of how to manage rapid, transformational whole system change in our recent book *Coherence: The Right Drivers in Action for Schools, Districts, and Systems* (Fullan & Quinn, 2016). We developed this framework by working with thousands of educators at all levels of the system. Once again, the ideas came via the interaction of practice and theory. The need for coherence resonated intuitively across the globe as a strategy to respond to the compliance-driven mandates, silos, overload, fragmentation, and continuous churn for policy makers and leaders that abounds in organizations today. Coherence provides an agile, organic framework that helps leaders integrate and strategize a transformational *whole system* change strategy and offers a pathway to make deep learning a reality.

Coherence by our definition is *the shared depth of understanding about the nature of the work.* The definition has two important components. The first is that coherence is fully subjective and thus cannot be explained by leaders or even strategic plans but must be developed through common experience. Second, because it exists in people's minds, it must be developed across given groups through purposeful interaction, working on a common agenda, identifying and consolidating what works, and making meaning over time. Coherence making is cumulative and is ongoing because people come and go, context shifts, and new ideas emerge. Coherence makers work to eliminate distractors and to forge concerted action that grapples with the day-to-day issues while making breakthroughs. Coherence has three essential features: it focuses on whole system change—100% of schools or districts; it zeros in on pedagogy or the process of learning; and it always considers the causal pathways that result in measurable impact for all students.

> Coherence by our definition is the shared depth of understanding about the nature of the work.

We started this chapter with a quote referring to seeking simplicity in the face of complex problems. Our version can be called *simplexity*—a term we adapted from Jeff Kluger (2009). In this case, the question is how can we achieve greater coherence in dynamic systems. By working with practitioners in whole systems (states, provinces, countries), we developed the Coherence Framework depicted in Figure 3.1. The framework consists of four essential components that can be applied to the journey of deep learning. Having just four major pieces is the simple part; making them gel as a synergistic set is the complex part.

The coherence framework is not linear; rather the four components work in concert and feed off each other. You may want to think of the components as similar to the four chambers of the heart. All are essential for

Figure 3.1 • The Coherence Framework

Source: Fullan, M., & Quinn, J. (2016). *Coherence: The Right Drivers in Action for Schools, Districts, and Systems.* Thousand Oaks, CA: Corwin.

life, although each has a function on its own. In the coherence framework, leadership acts as a force that pumps the blood to the areas that need it most. Leaders thus serve as activators, connectors, and integrators of the four components.

Focusing Direction

The first component of the framework involves the moral imperative of all children learning. It focuses on the whole child taking into account whatever background or life circumstances the student represents. Focusing direction begins the process of building shared meaning and collective purpose, developing a specific strategy to achieve the purpose, and the change leadership that best mobilizes people. Competing priorities or lack of a precise strategy can serve as a distraction that causes confusion or inertia and threatens focused direction. People may not be convinced of the strategy at the outset, and/or may lack skill, or fear failure. Leaders must "participate as learners" and help figure out the way to find progress. This means setting directional vision—getting shared purpose in place and a strategy to guide the initial work rather than spending too much time formulating the vision in the absence of action. Focusing direction should be conceived of as getting the deep learning journey underway. This change sequence works because taking action on the vision, especially collaboratively, clarifies the vision by starting to put it into practice. Leaders need to use the second component to build collaborative cultures for purposeful action.

Cultivating Collaborative Cultures

Cultivating collaborative cultures works in tandem with focusing direction to develop a nonjudgmental culture of growth that fosters the capacity and processes for change. Innovation requires an environment that allows mistakes as long as the group is learning from them. Collaboration becomes not just collegiality but the cultivation of expertise so that everyone is focused on the collective purpose. This collaborative expertise is a powerful change strategy as leaders use the group to change the group. Leaders foster conditions where people learn from and with each other about specific problems and practices. Focusing direction and collaborative cultures bring clarity, purpose, and the means to go deeper but can be superficial unless the actions in each of those components is directed to deepening learning. Effective leaders participate as learners with others as they attempt collectively to move the organization forward.

Deepening Learning

The third component, deepening learning, recognizes that schools and systems that are effective focus relentlessly on the learning-teaching process. They pay attention to three key aspects. First they establish clarity about learning goals so that educators, families, and students develop a shared understanding of the kind of learning and learners they want to develop. Some focus on getting the foundational literacies in place, while others are tackling the deep learning agenda accelerated by the digital world. The second aspect of deepening learning involves building precision in pedagogical practices. Precision develops as educators create communities of collective inquiry to build their collaborative expertise. They identify the new learning capacities and build precision in the new pedagogies and practices. Third, schools and systems create conditions and processes so that teachers and leaders can build their capacity to use the new practices and shift from less effective to more effective approaches. These are crucial areas of expertise that teachers and leaders need whether the focus is on closing the gap, improving foundational literacy, or pursuing the deep learning agenda.

Securing Accountability

The fourth component of the coherence framework acknowledges that the way to deal with external accountability is to build internal accountability—the capacity to measure progress from the inside out. This happens when the group takes self and collective responsibility for performance and engages with the external accountability system. The conditions that favor internal accountability include: specific goals, transparency of practice and results, precision of action (not to be confused with prescription), nonjudgmentalism, commitment to assessing impact, acting on evidence to improve results, and engaging with the external accountability system. If one works on the first three components of the coherence framework—by focusing direction, cultivating collaborative cultures, and attending to deepening learning—the conditions for internal accountability become established, enabling the organization to contend with the external accountability system.

As schools, districts, and whole systems began to tackle the coherence agenda, they wanted to know more about how to deepen learning. The Coherence Framework provides an overarching frame for looking at innovation through the lens of whole system change. As our work in coherence and deep learning has been developing simultaneously, it has evolved to detail a whole system approach to fostering and propelling deep learning. While we are not yet seeing any state, province, or country that has moved to deep learning as a whole system, we are seeing some glimpses of what may be possible.

In this next section, we examine in detail how we have expanded this component of *deepening learning* into a framework with a set of tools and processes that accelerate and amplify the deepening learning process. We explore how the New Pedagogies for Deep Learning (NPDL) partnership draws on all four components of coherence to create a social movement to foster deep learning around the globe.

Making Deep Learning Coherent

Massive change to the status quo of traditional schooling is not a simple matter because it involves every level of the system and also because the environment is volatile and ever changing. It must be an ongoing process, and the change must occur at the macrolevel (whole system or society) and at the microlevel (individual and local). At the microlevel it means redefining the outcomes of learning, catalyzing new leadership, creating new environments and partnerships, developing new capacities to design and assess deep learning, as well as new ways of measuring and reporting growth. Given such complexity, how do we move from the traditional model of schooling—one of sort and select—to one that focuses on helping all young people flourish and develop the global competencies?

The NPDL global partnership is tackling this challenge of moving from fragmented sites of innovation to pervasive transformation by building knowledge of the practices that deepen learning and the conditions that foster deep change in whole systems. Members of the partnership join because they have an interest in developing deep learning and want to learn from and with others on the same journey. This work is about regular school systems changing the culture of the district and its schools to go deeper for all children. It's taking the best of what we know about learning and whole system change and using that to create a process for changing learning in every school and classroom. For the past 4 years we have been immersed in the factors that facilitate or hinder the movement toward deep learning in systems, schools, and classrooms. Interacting with everyone ranging from students to policy makers, we are learning a lot about transformation and causing a shift in practice that we could not have imagined.

Our aim is not simply to describe the NPDL initiative and then suggest it be scaled up, but rather to identify the practices and principles that are leading to success. These clues and common threads about how and why it works can then inform what it will take to transform learning for all and feed into future practice. We have captured these in the Deep Learning Framework.

A Framework for Deep Learning

Such massive transformation from traditional to deep learning calls for a model that can guide action without constraining it, that is comprehensive but not unwieldy. We set out with our partners to catalyze and enable a social movement to help scores of schools, districts, and systems become immersed in developing cultures of deep learning.

Simply mobilizing action is not the whole story because all change is not good. One of our colleagues is the New Zealand school improvement expert Viviane Robinson. We especially like Viviane because she refuses to accept vague assertions, and instead insists on specific designs and

> We developed a Deep Learning Framework that intentionally details how the proposed change will produce the intended outcome, provides structures and processes that ensure the capacity to make the changes at all levels, and defines the change improvement regarding impact on learners.

explanations about change events. Her latest book, *Reduce Change to Increase Improvement* (2017), is no exception. As she puts it:

> By making the distinction between change and improvement, we increase leaders' responsibility for developing and communicating the detailed logic of how their proposed change will produce the intended improvement. (p. 3)

Accordingly, we developed a Deep Learning Framework that intentionally details how the proposed change will produce the intended outcome, provides structures and processes that ensure the capacity to make the changes at all levels, and defines the change improvement regarding impact on learners. The theory of action or causal pathway of NPDL is described in Figure 3.2. If the outcome we want is for all students to be deep learners, then we must ask, "What causes deep learning to be attained by all?"

Figure 3.2 • Deep Learning Framework

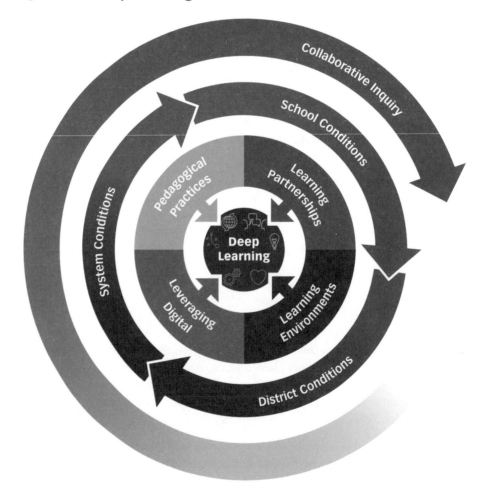

Source: Copyright © 2014 by New Pedagogies for Deep Learning™ (NPDL)

Working backwards, we see three key components. First, there must be clarity about the learning goals and what it means to be a deep learner. Second, it will only be fostered across all classrooms if we can define the learning process that makes it easy for teachers, leaders, students, and families to shift their thinking and practices. Third, it will only happen in whole schools and systems if we create the conditions for innovation, growth, and a culture of learning for all.

The deep learning framework supports the rapid spread of deep learning with a suite of tools and processes that can be adapted to fit the varied contexts of schools, districts, and systems and yet provides concrete ways to shift practice. Figure 3.2 depicts the four layers of the Deep Learning Framework as circles of support. Put as simply as possible and working backwards from the outcomes:

> Layer 1: Deep learning, defined as the **6Cs**, is the intended outcome.
>
> Layer 2: The **four elements of learning design** (practices, partnerships, environments, and digital) focus on developing the instructional experiences to accomplish the outcomes.
>
> Layer 3: **Conditions for deep learning** rubrics support schools, districts, and systems to foster deep learning.
>
> Layer 4: **Collaborative inquiry** surrounds the whole enterprise because deep learning requires continual learning at all levels.

Layer 1: Six Global Competencies for Deep Learning

The first circle of support at the center of the framework is deep learning, which is represented by the six global competencies: character, citizenship, creativity, critical thinking, collaboration, and communication. We define deep learning as *the process of acquiring these six global competencies*, also known as the 6Cs. These competencies describe the increasing complexity of thinking and problem solving, sophistication of collaborative skills, self-knowledge, and responsibility that underlies character and the ability to feel empathy and take action that makes one a global citizen. Building clarity about the learning outcomes in this layer is necessary if teachers, students, and families are to build common language and expectations. To measure progress we developed a more robust set of attributes and skills for each competency and tools called *learning progressions*.

Layer 2: Four Elements of Deep Learning Design

The second layer of the framework supports the learning design process. The four elements foster better learning design by bringing intentionality and precision to the integration of *pedagogical practices, learning partnerships, learning environments,* and *leveraging digital.* Teachers and students are paying attention to these four elements to ensure that learning experiences incorporate the complexity and depth that facilitates growth and scaffolds the prerequisite skills and understandings to maximize success. As well, the elements lead to intentionality in building new relationships between and among teachers, students, and families and using digital to facilitate and amplify learning. Specific tools, including a *Teacher Self-Assessment Diagnostic, Learning Design Rubric,* and *Learning Design Protocol*, support teachers to create learning experiences steeped in each element of the new pedagogies.

Layer 3: Conditions That Mobilize Deep Learning

Deep learning shouldn't be left to just a few innovative teachers, principals, and schools, so the third layer or circle of support describes the conditions that mobilize deep learning to spread exponentially across schools and systems. This set of conditions pertains to the whole system at three levels: school, district or cluster, and state. The question is what policies, strategies, and actions best foster the development of the 6Cs and four elements of the deep learning design. Frankly, this takes us into complex territory, and we have been busy defining and developing the best versions of how to depict and support the development of these push-and-pull change factors. We are still working on the precise formulation. For now, we can think of five core conditions that would need to be present at each of the three levels (school, cluster or district, and state): **vision, leadership, collaborative cultures, deepening learning,** and **new measures/assessment**. Note that these end up being parallel to the four components of the Coherence Framework (direction, collaboration, precision in pedagogy, accountability, and leadership at the core). The rubrics for the five conditions can be used to identify strengths, areas of improvement, guides to improvement, and assessment of progress.

Layer 4: Collaborative Inquiry Process

Finally, the framework's outer circle depicts a collaborative inquiry process that grounds the work and fosters the interaction effect of all layers. While it is pictured as the outer circle, it is not a final step but rather permeates each circle by creating powerful conversations at every stage of development. The collaborative inquiry process may be used by teachers to design deep learning experiences, by teams to moderate student work and growth, and by teachers and leaders to assess the conditions needed to foster deep learning at the school and system levels.

Final Thoughts

It's not a matter of working through each of the circles of support in sequence but rather having an understanding of the parts and how they intersect and reinforce one another interdependently—this is the synergy of the circles of support. The model is dynamic and thus ramifies making the whole greater than the sum of its parts. The final circle of collaboration is key because it drives the *learning from the work* process. Collaborative examination of practices unleashes the power of contagion and mutual help by generating new knowledge and ideas that mobilize action synergistically. The challenge lies next in building the shared purpose and collaborative expertise to release the powerful mindset that together students, teachers, and families can transform learning.

Section II digs more deeply into each layer of the Deep Learning Framework by drawing on the experience of our NPDL schools, districts, clusters, and systems. We do this to share the practices and elements that are leading to a whole system movement to transform the learning process. We invite you to use our framework to find your own entry point. The six chapters in Section II examine the deep learning framework in action: portraying deep learning (Chapter 4); designing it (Chapters 5 and 6); enabling it through collaboration (Chapter 7); NPDL as whole system change (Chapter 8); and new measures to assess it (Chapter 9).

SECTION II
The Living Laboratory

" I said, 'Somebody should do something about that.' Then I realized I am somebody. "

—LILY TOMLIN

Chapter 4

DEEP LEARNING IN ACTION

Deep Learning as a Force for Change

The centerpiece of the deep learning model is the 6Cs: character, citizenship, collaboration, communication, creativity, and critical thinking (Figure 4.1).

Figure 4.1 • Deep Learning Competencies

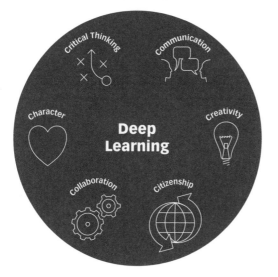

Are these competencies the right ones? Are they the only ones? Will they be the same ones in 2 years or 5 years or 10? Worldwide skills lists for the future proliferate as organizations and educators scramble to get it right. Figure 4.2 captures lists of skills that may be needed by future workforces gleaned from recent reports by the Apollo Institute, The World Economic Forum ("Institute for the Future," 2011), and New Pedagogies for Deep Learning (NPDL).

Comparing the lists to our six competencies, the commonalities and congruence emerge as well as the trends. The nuances will be continually

Figure 4.2 • **The Future of Work**

Apollo Institute 2020	World Economic Forum 2015	World Economic Forum 2020	NPDL
1. Sense making	1. Complex problem solving	1. Complex problem solving	1. Character
2. Social intelligence	2. Coordinating with others	2. Critical thinking	2. Citizenship
3. Novel and adaptive thinking	3. People management	3. Creativity	3. Communication
4. Cross cultural competency	4. Critical thinking	4. People management	4. Collaboration
5. Computational thinking	5. Negotiation	5. Coordinating with others	5. Critical thinking
6. New media literacy	6. Quality control	6. Emotional intelligence	6. Creativity
7. Transdisciplinary	7. Service orientation	7. Judgment and decision making	
8. Design mindset	8. Judgment and decision making	8. Service orientation	
9. Cognitive load management	9. Active listening	9. Negotiation	
10. Virtual collaboration	10. Creativity	10. Cognitive flexibility	

Source: Grey, A. (2016). *The 10 Skills You Need to Thrive in the Fourth Industrial Revolution.* World Economic Forum. Retrieved from https://www.weforum.org/agenda/2016/01/the-10-skills-you-need-to-thrive-in-the-fourth-industrial-revolution.

evolving. The world economic forum article suggests that creativity will become one of the top three skills because of the avalanche of new technologies, products, and ways of working that will require new capacities. They envision negotiation and flexibility moving higher on future lists and note the emergence of emotional intelligence.

In our work, we see creativity rising in prominence and becoming a catalyst for development of the other Cs. At the same time, compassion and empathy as dimensions of character and citizenship are increasingly prominent because everyone struggles to deal with diverse challenges and perspectives that are more prevalent in a complex world. Definitive answers on the perfect set of competencies are not known, but we are focusing on six broad competencies that give learners the ability to learn for life, be agile, be in tune with their evolving world, and be the kind of human beings the world needs. The most important thing we can do is focus on bringing the competencies to life while being proactive to adjusting based on changing needs.

We see creativity rising in prominence and becoming a catalyst for development of the other Cs.

CHAPTER 4

These new deep learning competencies can be an elusive concept, so let's step inside a few classrooms around the globe to see what's actually different about this kind of learning that fosters the growth of the 6Cs.

In **Finland,** we join teacher Tarja Kohlmann at the Kirkkojarvi School as she describes the new approach to learning.

Finnish Students Tackle Climate Change

Tarja Kohlmann, Primary School Teacher; Espoo, Finland

In Finland, we want to provide the best learning environment possible. We have a beautiful modern building, but with the new Finnish curriculum introduced this year and our work in NPDL we are becoming a learning community focused on what matters. Teachers are collaborating, and the learning experiences for students are much different than the old ways of teaching. Students are currently engaged in a deep challenge around climate change. Students in the primary school are excited because they don't know much at first and must gather the information to evaluate the problem and then find solutions. We encourage them to dig deeper by contacting experts and interacting with other students and families in new ways. We see this way of learning is sparking the imagination of students as they implement their solutions, look at the results, and reflect on their work. Students use a collaborative platform to connect and capture their progress, so I see their trials and triumphs right in front of me. Learning this way, the students are supported to think about their role as global citizens, critical consumers of information, communicators, and collaborators, and this enables creative and deep learning. They are building character traits that will allow them to go into the world and make learning an internal part of life.

To learn more about how teachers and students are using partnerships and leveraging digital to transform learning, visit **www.npdl.global** and view Video 4.1, Finnish Students Tackle Climate Change.

online resources

Across the globe in **Uruguay** a program to provide devices to all students so that they could be part of the global community was initiated 7 years ago. Uruguay is noteworthy because it is a poor country that has moved quickly on a large scale by adopting inexpensive adaptive technology and software linked to improvements in teaching and learning in relation to local and world problems. Leaders soon realized that deeper pedagogy was needed to activate the potential of the digital devices, so Uruguay joined the NPDL partnership. Let's visit a classroom to glimpse what is possible when pedagogy and digital are combined. Soledad and Claudia, 11-year-old students from Montevideo, share their story of how they investigated new ways of learning and engaging their classmates in adventures that impact real issues in their world.

Unleashing Learning With Robotics

Primary School Students; Montevideo, Uruguay

Soledad and Claudia wanted to explore the world around them but felt trapped in a classroom that was the same every day. They worked diligently, but each day their attention was riveted on the boxes stacked in the corner of the room. They asked the teacher repeatedly to let them explore the boxes and kits but were not allowed to touch. One day their teacher told them she was learning about a new way of teaching so she was trying new methods in the classroom. She was also connecting to teachers in other schools, cities, and even other countries. The girls once again begged to explore the kits, and this time the teacher said yes! Within 2 hours the girls had sorted and organized the contents of the boxes and kits and watched videos on the YouTube channel, where they learned how to assemble and program a robot. Once their classmates saw the first robot, they also wanted to be part of exploring.

The next challenge they set for themselves was to connect green technology and robotics so they could build a robot that could solve problems for humanity. One group of students was learning about war and built a robot that could detect land mines. Soon they began to think of solving problems nearer home. They remembered that last year, five people, including a 10-year-old boy, had died from lightning on the beaches of Montevideo, so they researched lightning and built a warning device that sets off an alarm so people know when lightning may strike. Excitement spread as groups began to think of other ways to impact their own community and the world with the robots. Parents started to get involved because younger children were excited to take part but needed help. The interest was so high that Soledad and Claudia created a team of students who could help others. The teacher describes a new relationship with students: "We are partners." Students see a new learning process, and then they "suggest projects or topics and the teacher helps them to improve." Soon students wanted to challenge themselves more, so the teacher introduced them to the learning progressions and rubrics she had learned about in her work with NPDL. The students now say this is the best part because they have choices in the work and they can use the tools to improve the learning and measure their progress. They have learned to create for the world, to use their minds, and to protect and change their world.

To learn more about this classroom's journey to deep learning, view Video 4.2, Global Learning Network: Deep Learning With Robotics, at **www.npdl.global**.

online resources

Next we step into a high school classroom in **Ontario, Canada**, where Grade 12 students studying World Issues Geography are engaging in an analysis of the influence of government, groups, and individuals on the management of social change.

Bringing the UN Goals for Sustainability to Life

Grade 12 Students; Ontario, Canada

Grade 12 students were challenged to educate others about the UN Sustainability Goals and to prompt people to take local and global action. Students formed teams based on interest then connected, partnered, and engaged with environmental organizations such as the World Wildlife Fund and Friends of Earth as well as social agencies such as Me to We, local food banks, and Feed the Children. Students cocreated the success criteria and learning goals, tweeted their progress regularly to family and community, and created a blog to reach their intended audience and encourage further partnerships. Impacts on real action included organizing a *Because I Am a Girl* event at a local elementary school, coordinating a blood donor drive, developing a documentary on poverty and facilitating a community awareness event @poverty2power, making and selling shirts to help young people go to school, building furniture and giving the proceeds to Friends of Earth, and supporting a sustainable consumption initiative. Students say as a result, "We are learning to think outside the box . . . learning to take risks" and "dreaming as big as we can." Their teacher notes, "The most rewarding part was watching my students become empowered and passionate about their chosen goal and . . . eager to learn, share and make a change in the world."

Not only can we see then that the 6Cs are pursued in different ways, but we also observe that there are commonalities. When parents, students, and educators watch these videos or read the passages, they often notice:

- students are excited and deeply engaged in contributing to each other and to humanity;

- new relationships for learning between and among students, teachers, families, and communities emerge;

- complex collaboration, creativity, and problem solving develop;

- "school" is extended to include other spaces, time, and expert connections; and

- the critical thinking necessary to tackle these real-life issues blossoms.

One could simply ascribe these characteristics to a good problem-based or inquiry model. While deep learning may frequently use those teaching models and many other powerful ones, inquiry or problem-based learning (PBL) are *not* synonyms for deep learning. All three examples involve students learning independently and collaboratively. Deep learning is thus the process that causes students to use more complex thinking, to tap into creativity, and to solve increasingly enigmatic problems. Students can use the inquiry model for intricate tasks with or without collaborating. At other times we want to intentionally develop collaboration, so that means we need discrete opportunities for meaningful group-based learning tasks, and then models such as problem-based and cooperative group learning are useful. Deep learning is not about one particular model of teaching, but is fostered by a wide range of learning practices. As one school leader noted:

> It's like having a big circle framed by the 6Cs. Inside the circle are the pedagogical approaches that will help kids flourish but we get to choose. So if my school is into design thinking that fits but if another school is using inquiry or problem based models then that works also. The good news is that we get to select the approaches that are right for our students and community. We have lots of choice but with that comes the responsibility for making wise choices based on good data and knowledge. (personal communication, July 2017)

What is distinctive is that regardless of the models of teaching used, this type of learning accelerates the acquisition of the six global competencies or 6Cs—character, citizenship, collaboration, communication, creativity, and critical thinking.

Emerging Discoveries

One of the most exciting findings has been the unbridled optimism of students, teachers, and leaders who describe a renewed energy, passion, and liberation. We hypothesize that this is due in part to the greater voice and choice this kind of learning engenders. As the learning becomes more grounded in real life, we are observing new behaviors. A much greater intentionality and precision emerges as teachers define deep learning outcomes; select from new and powerful pedagogies; codesign with students giving them both choice and voice; measure the effect of learning experiences and pedagogical practices on student deep learning; and recognize digital as a ubiquitous element of learning that facilitates connections to a universe of ideas, experts, collaborators, and possibilities. This intentionality of practice leads to new roles, new relationships, and new learning partnerships. All this is occurring within an environment that fosters innovation, values individual interests and talents, and connects to real life authentically so that learning is not a preparation for tomorrow but is life—today. Here are some of the discoveries we are making.

Helping Humanity

Students have a commitment to making a difference and contributing to the betterment of the world. Whether they are the students we met from Uruguay who are building a warning system to anticipate lightning on the beaches, or the high school students bringing the UN goals for

One of the most exciting findings has been the unbridled optimism of students, teachers, and leaders who describe a renewed energy, passion, and liberation.

sustainability to life in their local communities and globally, we see students taking action. While the 21st century skills of communication, collaboration, creativity, and critical thinking dominated the discussion for the past two decades, we are seeing character and citizenship take a giant step forward. And until now, creativity has never been prominent in schools, as Sir Ken Robinson (2015) has so eloquently and relentlessly argued.

Overall our deep learners are thinking like global citizens, considering global issues based on a deep understanding of diverse values and worldviews, and with a genuine interest and ability to solve ambiguous and complex real-world problems that impact human and environmental sustainability. At the same time they are tackling real-life problems, they are developing the personal qualities of grit, tenacity, perseverance, empathy, compassion, and resilience and honing the ability to make learning an integral part of living. We like the 10-year-old girl in Uruguay who said, "I am supposed to help humanity so I decided to start with my own neighborhood." Or the hordes of students who in effect say, "I don't want to wait 10 years to be a citizen. I want to be a citizen of tomorrow today. The world needs me!" All this augurs well for the future: a win-win for students and humankind alike.

> We like the 10-year-old girl in Uruguay who said, "I am supposed to help humanity so I decided to start with my own neighborhood."

Students as Agents of Change

Students have untapped potential, but given voice and choice through deep learning we see them influencing dramatic changes to organizations, society, and pedagogy.

Organizations

Amazing results emerged when Glashan Middle School, in **Ottawa, Canada**, made a bold decision about student leadership:

Student Voice Leads the Learning

Middle School Students; Ottawa, Canada

The school's deep learning journey began with an invitation to students to become part of a Deep Learning Design Team. These students in Grades Seven and Eight took on leadership roles in helping develop a common understanding and set of goals to build deeper learning across their school. On a recent visit it was clear that students were integral to the shift to deep learning. We met with 25 members of the student team, who were able to articulate with specificity and examples how the 6Cs were informing their choices in their learning and also developing them as human beings ready for life. One example of the pervasiveness of the 6Cs in the school culture

(Continued)

relates to a student trip to Sweden in May 2017, limited to 12 students (as we saw in the vignette in Chapter 1). Faced with tough decisions on the criteria for selection, they developed a challenge for students to create something based on the 6Cs that illustrated why they should be chosen. The results ranged from a suitcase filled with all the student accomplishments based on the 6Cs to poster boards and scrapbooks detailing the student's use of the 6Cs.

Teachers are of course an integral part of this shift to deep learning at Glashan, but it is clear that unleashing the creativity and talent of student leadership amplified impact.

> Students have untapped potential, but given voice and choice through deep learning we see them influencing dramatic changes to organizations, society, and pedagogy.

Society

As students contribute to their local and global communities, they begin to rethink their place not only in learning but also in changing their world. They push against the traditional structures of schooling by asking "why" and "why not." When they are engaged in meaningful, relevant tasks, they see few limits.

Speed Dating With the Pollies

Year 12 Students; Victoria, Australia

Students at Bendigo Senior Secondary College arranged a preelection forum, with local political candidates and community members, titled Speed Dating with the Pollies. Year 12 applied learning students at Bendigo Senior Secondary College were first-time voters in the 2016 federal election, and they were nervous and confused about local, national, and global issues. They organized an event where students from their school could meet local political candidates, question them about a range of issues, and then make well-informed choices when they voted in the federal election. Students invited the mayor to be part of their organizing committee; they met with a variety of community groups, sourced policy information from each of the candidates, and created a show-bag for first-time voters in the lead up to their "Speed Dating with the Pollies" event. Students felt at the center of something important, and they were listening to the talk, the issues, and the arguments they had channeled to their school. Students found that the media wanted to know what they thought! Students' citizenship and skills developed by stealth. Although students thought they were just involved in organizing a big event, through that experience, they were exposed to ideas, language, opposing arguments, and challenging questions.

Community involvement far exceeded expectations, with local private schools asking to attend the event and parents sending questions to be

CHAPTER 4

Students saw that they can play a role in mobilizing community awareness and action.

Pedagogy

Once students engage in this authentic learning that matters, they are less willing to go back to worksheets and textbooks. They have no attachment to the status quo and therefore are ready for change. They are an unexpected "push" factor for teachers to change. Because teachers see student transform before their eyes, they are motivated to take more risks themselves. This new learning partnership is helping teachers and students push the edges of learning in ways the teachers alone could not have predicted, as illustrated in an interview by CBC radio with teachers and students at Bessborough School in **New Brunswick**:

Sweat Equity: The Plant Garden

Grade Six Students; New Brunswick, Canada

The drop off zone in front of the school has been transformed into a sweat equity and plant science garden containing 20 varieties of non-GMO organic fruits and vegetables as well as three bee pollinator friendly gardens. All were researched and designed by Grade Six students. Teachers had become involved in the NPDL partnership a few months before and wanted to engage their students in thinking about local, community, and global issues. Teachers thought about bees because a third of food comes from plants pollinated by them. Once the idea was introduced that they might take action, the ideas from students were flying so much they wanted to work through recess. Students did research then chose a medium to present their work, including: Minecraft to create a tour of a beehive; Toontastic 3D, a creative storytelling app; building 3D models such as a bee hotel; and coding Spheros, an app-enabled robotic ball to replicate the bee world. They held a bee showcase to share their findings with parents. Teachers recount examples of students who used to have chronic absenteeism but are now showing up every day. When asked why, they said it was the bee project. Other students who attend regularly but are not very engaged were totally engaged because they got to choose and wanted to be part of something that raised awareness. "My role of the teacher changed—students had the ideas and I encouraged advised and gave tips but it was a collaborative effort." The collaboration spread to include grades above and below and drew on the expertise of a world-renowned bee-keeper. As one student said, "I was surprised by what kind of hard stuff you can do. . . . When they said we could save the bees, I said I want to do it!"

CHAPTER 4

Students brought a range of new pedagogies from the digital world as they investigated how they could share their findings and take action. The collaboration pushed new thinking about what school looks like and what happens to help students learn.

The Equity Hypothesis

We proposed in earlier chapters our equity hypothesis that all students need deep learning but that those who have been underserved in traditional schooling may need it even more. Here we provide only two examples out of many we could have selected. The first example illustrates that when students pursue deep learning in areas of relevance to their own lives, they not only improve in academic areas, but also find their place and voice.

Students Find Their Voice

Sam, High School Student; Ontario, Canada

For students from poverty backgrounds, deep learning can be a life-changing experience, because they begin to sense the power to direct their own lives and improve the lives of others. This is the case for the following First Nation student.

Sam was struggling in high school in Timmins, Ontario. Leaving his indigenous community and culture behind, as well as his grandmother with whom he lived, traveling hundreds of miles away to attend school in a community where many people expected First Nations youth to fail, boarding with a family he didn't know, he was beginning to understand why so many students from his village gave up and dropped out of school. A teacher engaged students in his class in a program called Students as Researchers, sponsored by the Ontario government. Sam was academically behind others in his class but wanted to take part because students got to work in a team to choose an area they would be interested in researching and improving. He talked to a few other students from his indigenous community, and soon they had a group. Their research question: What are the experiences of indigenous youth when they transition to high school? They designed surveys and interview questions and gathered their evidence from students who had survived the transition and graduated, students who had dropped out, elders in their own community, students and staff in their school, and members of families who provided room and board to indigenous students when they came to the city. By the end of the course they completed their report, a litany of challenges and barriers ranging from loneliness to racism, to feelings of hopelessness and failure.

And they knew what they needed to do. Sam and his group wanted to use their report to fuel a change, and they became passionately committed to ensuring that young people from their community have a different experience. With the support of their school and some of the elders of their community, they formed an Aboriginal Youth Advisory Committee at their school. This council gave indigenous youth a voice and allowed the students to lead the changes needed in their school: indigenous mentors, peer tutoring, activities designed to celebrate indigenous cultural events and history for both indigenous and nonindigenous students, and steps taken to change the host family experiences and connections to the community. What began as a project within a single course became a multiyear transition and action plan for indigenous students and a shift in understanding within the entire school. Sam changed from a shy young man lacking literacy skills who counselors recommended pursue courses in the applied track, to a confident young man who enjoyed reading and research, worked as a youth counselor at a Native Friendship Centre, and aspired to a university program leading to a teaching certification (Fullan & Gallagher, 2017).

The second example shows what happens when a student usually assigned to lower-level classes gets an opportunity to pursue something of personal interest.

Make Learning Relevant: Unleash the Passion

Gabe, Secondary Student; Ontario, Canada

Gabe is a secondary student who usually enrolled in classes that were delivered for the workplace "applied stream." However, he recently joined an academic course in kinesiology because he loved sports and had a strong connection to the teacher, who encouraged him to take the course. Through her participation in a school-based inquiry around deep learning, Gabe's teacher had redesigned many of her learning tasks to allow students more choice on what they learned and how they demonstrated their understanding of the curriculum expectations. Gabe's teacher had her students apply their learning to a real-world context as often as they could. The result was that Gabe, who has learning challenges, could access the curriculum. As an example of such a deep learning task, the students were to explore the nutrition needs of an elite sport of their choosing and create a nutrition supplement from all-natural ingredients that would help athletes prepare and recover from intense competition. During a class marketing forum, students had to promote their nutrition product to industry experts whom they had invited into their class to receive feedback. Community members such as a former professional hockey player, Cross Fit gym owner, a runner who recently completed the Boston Marathon, and a personal trainer for elite swimmers sampled their products and asked

(Continued)

(Continued)

students questions about their learning. Through this deep learning task, Gabe surprised himself and his teacher with his commitment to his learning. Gabe was able to apply his learning about important nutrients and calories and connect it to his passion for basketball. When asked, Gabe explained that he was able to learn deeply about this topic because he was asked to learn about something he was passionate about. Gabe reflected that because he was asked to demonstrate his learning in a creative way, through designing a product, he felt more engaged and confident. He said that if he was asked to complete a test, he would have had less interest and not have been able to demonstrate the depth of his learning. Gabe also explained that he was proud of his work and felt like he could learn alongside peers in a way that he had not been able to before.

Deep learning is inclusive for all. Deep learning instills confidence and perseverance, and provides opportunities for all students to succeed, despite the learning challenges perceived by others or by the individual themselves. We do not claim that equity can be attained in the short run but that moving toward that outcome should be the aspirational goal of systems. And when equity and excellence are linked with policies and strategies that address the health and safety needs of students, the combination can be powerful.

Measuring impact in the new domain of global competencies is a challenge, but we see promise in the work of our Finnish colleague Pasi Sahlberg (Rubin, 2016), who differentiates between "big" and "small" data. He describes *big data* as consisting of massive data sets of information about a complex range of indicators that cannot be processed by conventional applications. While extensive, they do not give decision makers deep understanding of what good teaching is and how it is leading to better learning. Sahlberg points to the work of Martin Lindstrom (2016) and his term *small data* as more promising. *Small data* refers to small clues that uncover huge trends. The small clues are often woven into the fabric of the schools, so we are gathering small data in the form of case vignettes and examples where students who have been floundering in traditional schooling are flourishing in deep learning environments.

We can all point to stories where students find success despite challenges. What is different here is that we are not drawing from isolated pockets of success but are seeing this type of learning transformation across our deep learning schools. As noted, we are using the small data concept to gather powerful vignettes that ramify when considered in total. Deep learning is causing more disconnected students to become engaged. They become more likely to participate because learning is geared to each and every student. It becomes the norm for the critical mass of peers and up and down the organization. This deeper engagement and accelerated progress result from the increased specificity of the learning outcomes, the focus of the six competencies, and the deep learning experiences that are fostered. This equity hypothesis can have a profound impact on policy and whole system change because the mindset shifts from one of deficits and fixing broken students to one of growth and unleashing potential.

Making Deep Learning Come Alive

Transformational changes—social movements—are about ideas that move people to action, not rhetoric. No amount of proclaiming, moralizing, or advocating is likely to make people shift their practice. What we have found is that seeing examples of students who are changing the way they think, feel, and interact with the world is a more powerful influencer. The next best thing to seeing your own students change is to see videos or movies of authentic deep learning in action. We have included numerous stories of change throughout the book and also links to video because the digital world brings the experience to life. If you think you and others in your school or district may ready to explore deep learning, we offer three suggestions for getting started.

1. Promote Powerful Conversations

Students, teachers, leaders, and parents need time to get their heads around the new concepts and ideas, so they need opportunities to have deep discussions about what they want for students. You may want to organize role-alike groups and then build momentum toward a joint sharing of ideas and understanding. Whether the group consists of principals beginning to think about change in the school, an entire school staff envisioning the future, or a mixed group of educators, families, and community members, using video examples is a compelling way to bring out a variety of perspectives through deep dialogue. Using a protocol as an organizer that guides the conversation can facilitate the group to explore their similarities and differences productively and then to reach a consensus on a collective vision of what they want for the learners. Having a protocol that uses key questions or the 6Cs as an organizer ensures that all voices are heard, relationships are deepened, and shared understanding and focus result. Consider sharing a video that stimulates peers to think about what might be possible for students in the global, digital world. You may want use videos identified in this book or examples of innovative classrooms found on sites such as Edutopia, Expeditionary Learning (EL Education), or YouTube. As participants discuss what excited them about the video and the type of learning that they saw, they begin to develop a shared definition of deep learning and what it looks like in practice. Link the competencies and the new ways of learning to your context by having the groups identify the ways the school and/or district is already developing these kinds of learners. Challenge teachers and leaders to think about one thing they could do to make learning deeper in their own classroom and school and then take action on it. Be sure to invite them to share the successes at a specific future date.

2. Cultivate a Culture of Deep Learning

If deep learning is to take root and flourish, everyone must see himself or herself as a learner. Leaders can pave the way by creating opportunities for rich dialogue and creating conditions where people feel they can risk trying something new. What is needed is a culture that invites participation, that engages creativity and diversity of thought, and where learning from and with one another is a habit. Leaders shape the culture of learning when they *model* by being learners themselves, *monitor* the relationships and learning culture, and then *measure* growth and celebrate successes. Across the globe, teacher leadership is on the ascendance. They describe feeling liberated to teach what really matters in a way that makes sense: "This is the reason I came into teaching." "I used to think that inquiry wouldn't allow me to cover the curriculum in Grade Six. Now I think that inquiry actually allows the curriculum to be uncovered."

Here are two examples of how teachers are creating a similar culture of learning for the students. First we see how one teacher has helped students build a deep understanding of the 6Cs that impact life inside the classroom and beyond.

In a diverse classroom in Toronto, Canada, the bulletin board is titled "We're not good until we're all good." The title of each of the 6Cs are scattered across the board. Early in the year students created I WONDER sticky notes about what others in the class might achieve this year and placed them next to a competency; for example, *I wonder if Jason will become an artist because he's the best in our school* (the narrator explains that Jason created his own action comic drawings for a recent project). As the year progresses, students take time at the end of each day to reflect on evidence of the 6Cs and add sticky notes to the wall documenting these accomplishments. The result is a living wall of the evidence of growth.

This is a powerful strategy because two things happen. Students build a shared understanding of what competencies look like and sound like (e.g., they articulated the dimensions of collaboration moving from simple teamwork to deep appreciation of skills each brings to the task now); and a culture of reflection and appreciation emerges that is owned by the students as they develop skill in looking for evidence points, self-regulating, and developing a mindset that seeks and celebrates growth.

In another classroom, the teacher has introduced a student version of the learning progressions. At the beginning, students use the progression to self-assess and set a personal goal for the next deep learning challenge. Over time, students develop skills in giving and receiving feedback and use the student progression as an anchor for those discussions and as a method for collecting evidence of growth. Some teachers introduce only one competency at a time while others use one or more. To learn more about the growth that is possible as students develop competency in giving feedback by focusing on the Cs of collaboration and communication, view Video 4.3, Writing Conference: Peer Feedback, at **www.npdl.global**.

What we see happening is that a collective understanding of the 6Cs emerges as a living part of the culture. Students begin to act more ethically and with greater empathy in their interactions with peers and the world. But it's not just about feeing good—a depth of intentionality begins to emerge both in the way the teacher designs and codesigns learning using the progressions as an anchor and on the part of students to develop themselves and to see that growth in others.

3. Think Big—Start Small

The journey to deep learning is just that—a journey. There is no one pathway. If we want to influence this shift as leaders, we need to model it, monitor the change, and measure impact.

Leaders model when they identify deep learning as a valued goal and invest in developing personal understanding, develop ways to build collective understanding of the 6Cs, and select videos that model deep learning. Ask participants to observe and record evidence of ways the students are developing the 6Cs. Discuss the kinds of learning processes that seem to foster the acquisition of these competencies. Challenge teachers to take an existing lesson or unit they will teach in the next 2 weeks and be intentional using one of the competencies. If teaching a history unit, think about how they could ask questions that would increase the complexity of critical thinking by the students. If teaching writing, think about how they could use peer feedback and be intentional about how they develop stronger collaboration skills in the students for that task.

Teachers and other leaders can monitor what is important, and celebrate early examples at meetings, professional learning sessions, and through visitations. They measure impact on the culture and students' outcomes and celebrate growth. In the course of this process, they sort out what is working and should be retained and further developed. In this way innovation and continuous improvement get built into the culture.

Final Thoughts

What we propose here is moving deep learning from the margins of practice for a few students or schools to being the foundation of learning for all—moving from bright spots of innovation to fostering this excitement and accomplishment with learners across the world. The big challenge lies in mobilizing such a shift in thinking and practice. It requires not simply a diffusion of innovation but an unleashing of potential—a transformation so that the highest hopes and promises are realized for all. We see this as an emerging *social movement* since it is evolving from the excitement and commitment of teachers, leaders, families, and students engaging in deep learning.

Building clarity and shared understanding of the competencies is the first step toward deep learning. Note that in Figure 4.2, when we compared our 6Cs with other lists, we had 6 key competencies while the other three all had 10. There is no magical number, but simplexity calls for the smallest number of mutually exclusive core factors that are essential for success. The core list must be comprehensive and memorable. Clarity of the competencies is foundational, but crafting deep learning experiences is crucial. To do this you need a framework to zero in on the core components. In Chapters 5 and 6, we examine the four elements of deep learning design.

> We propose moving deep learning from the margins of practice for a few students or schools to being the foundation of learning for all.

Notes

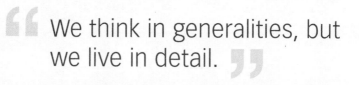

We think in generalities, but
we live in detail.

—ALFRED NORTH WHITEHEAD

Chapter 5

DESIGNING DEEP LEARNING

Learning Partnerships

The New Pedagogies

The need to fundamentally shift the process of learning is no longer a debate. Educators, families, policy makers, and society at large agree that students need new capacities to thrive today and in the future. The growth or acquisition of these competencies is the definition of *deep learning*. While there is accelerating agreement that learning must change, the challenge lies in *how* to foster these competencies and to do so for *all* students and in complex systems. As we spell out in this chapter, these developments call for a more comprehensive learning design and correspondingly new roles for students, families, teachers, and school leaders.

Building clarity and shared language between and among students, families, and educators mobilizes commitment and action to develop the competencies that allow all students to flourish. Once we have agreement on the learning outcomes—the global competencies—we need to ask, "How do we design learning environments and experiences that foster the acquisition of these competencies?" and "How do we get large numbers of teachers and students engaged in this new process for learning?" Our fourfold solution—the learning design elements—is displayed in Figure 5.1.

As we saw in Chapter 4, the process of establishing learning goals begins with an explicit focus on students' strengths and needs and uses the six global competencies (6Cs) as a lens for considering the curriculum content. The emphasis is on the big ideas and concepts that are being developed rather than minute facts and fragmented activities. Even when teachers are inspired to develop deep learning experiences and embrace the new pedagogies, they benefit from using an organizer that helps them consider the multiple aspects of complex learning. In practice, the four elements of the new pedagogies are integrated and mutually reinforcing. In the graphic, they are separated to accentuate the need to consider each in its own right, build precision in the interrelationships, and increase intentionality in learning designs.

Figure 5.1 • Four Elements of Learning Design

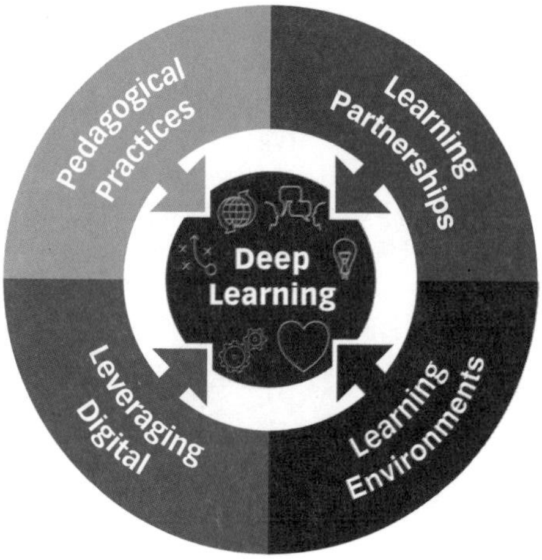

Source: Copyright © 2014 by New Pedagogies for Deep Learning™ (NPDL)

What Is New About the New Pedagogies

1. They focus on the *creation and use of new knowledge in the real world* rather than only transmitting knowledge that already exists.

2. They intentionally forge new learning partnerships between and among students and teachers, because the *learning process* becomes the focal point for the mutual discovery, creation, and use of knowledge.

3. New pedagogies *expand the learning environment* by moving beyond the traditional classroom walls to use time, space, and people within and beyond the classroom walls as a catalyst for building new knowledge and creating a robust culture for learning.

4. The new pedagogies *leverage digital ubiquitously* to accelerate and deepen the learning not simply as an add-on or end in itself.

The new pedagogies are in direct contrast to traditional teaching that focused more on content mastery, teacher-centered design, a transmission of information, and bolting on technology. In this chapter, we start with *learning partnerships* and in Chapter 6 move successively to learning environments, leveraging digital, and pedagogical practices. This time we have left pedagogy to the last so that the reader could appreciate the other three elements as larger and important parts of the overall learning design.

Learning Partnerships

Dramatically new learning relationships are emerging between and among students, teachers, families, and the external world. This shift in voice, control, and relationships is a distinctive feature of deep learning. Teachers are excited when describing the new teacher-student relationships where teachers are becoming *partners* in the learning with students. The impact of this type of learning on students is illustrated in their own words— "It's much easier to learn from our peers than a teacher at the front." "It's good to be connected to people beyond our town because it expands our horizons." "I'm putting this work out there because I'm proud of it and I want your feedback."

Learning partnerships, as depicted in Figure 5.2, is one of the four key design elements of the new pedagogies.

The new partnerships have significant potential to reframe learning by connecting learners to authentic opportunities locally, nationally, and globally. As learning becomes more relevant and authentic, it moves beyond the classroom walls and builds on student needs and interests more organically. This new focus on relationships is an accelerator for learning but does not happen by chance. It requires new roles of students, teachers, families, and communities in the learning process and ways to be intentional about fostering these new learning relationships.

Figure 5.2 • Learning Partnerships

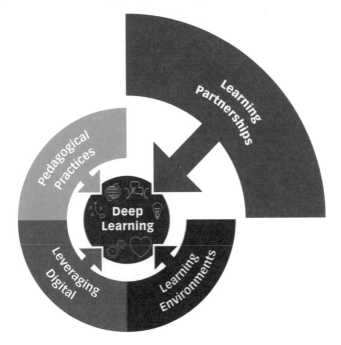

Source: Copyright © 2014 by New Pedagogies for Deep Learning™ (NPDL)

A New Role for Students

The new role for students goes beyond the notions of student voice and student agency to combine both internal development and external connections to the world. We are seeing a deeper engagement of students as co-designers and co-learners. Meaningful learning partnerships with students can be accelerated when teachers build on the three components of the student learning model to develop students as active, engaged learners who are prepared to learn for life and experience learning as life (see Figure 5.3).

> We are seeing a deeper engagement of students as co-designers and co-learners.

Figure 5.3 • Student Learning Model

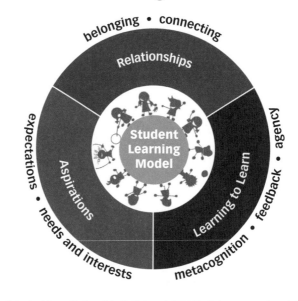

Source: Adapted from Fullan, M., & Quinn, J. (2016). *Coherence: The Right Drivers in Action for Schools, Districts, and Systems* (p. 94). Thousand Oaks, CA: Corwin.

Learning to Learn

Students need to take responsibility for their learning and to understand the process of learning, if it is to be maximized. This requires students to develop skills in *metacognition*, giving and receiving *feedback*, and enacting *student agency*.

- Learning to learn requires that students build metacognition about their learning and master the process of learning. They begin to define their own learning goals and success criteria; monitor their own learning; critically examine their work; and incorporate feedback from peers, teachers, and others to deepen their awareness of how they function in the learning process.

- Feedback is essential to improving performance. As students make progress in mastering the learning process, the role of the teacher gradually shifts from explicitly structuring the learning task, toward providing feedback, activating the next learning challenge, and continuously developing the learning environment.

- Student agency and autonomy emerges because students take a more active role in co-developing learning tasks and assessing results. It is more than participation; it is engaging students in real decision making and a willingness to learn together.

Relationships

The second element of relationships is a crucial foundation for all human beings who are social by nature and crave purpose, meaning, and connectedness to others (Ryan & Deci, 2017; Tough, 2016). Caring and connectedness in particular are critical:

- *Caring* environments help students flourish and meet the basic need of all humans to feel they are respected and belong. This sense of belonging is emerging as a powerful motivator as students seek to *help humanity*—locally and globally.

- *Connecting through meaningful relationships* is integral to authentic learning. As students develop both interpersonal connections and intrapersonal insight, they are able to move to successively more complex tasks in groups and independently. Managing collaborative relationships and being self-monitoring are skills for life.

Aspirations

Student results can be dramatically affected by the expectations they hold of themselves and the perceptions they believe others have for them (see also Quaglia & Corso, 2014; Robinson, 2015, 2017; Ryan & Deci, 2017; Tough, 2016).

- *Expectations* are a key determinant of success, as noted in Hattie's (2012) research. Students must believe they can achieve and also feel that others believe that. They must co-determine success criteria and be engaged in measuring their growth. Families, students, and teachers can together foster higher expectations through deliberate means—sometimes simply by discussing current and ideal expectations and what might make them possible to achieve.

- *Needs and interests* are a powerful accelerator for motivation and engagement. Teachers who tap into the natural curiosity and interest of students are able to use that as a springboard to deeply engage students in tasks that are relevant and authentic and examine concepts and problems in depth.

Linking learning to student aspirations, providing powerful feedback, and building on student curiosity and interest builds stronger co-learning partnerships that help teachers more deeply know their individual students and, through that, analyze student progress to understand which teaching and learning strategies best activate an individual student's learning. The learning partners—teachers and students—must find the right balance between structure and independence, and that balance will be unique to each learning context.

This shift toward more active, connected learning where students take greater charge of their own learning and each other's learning both inside and outside the classroom is described by a teacher in this way, "We've seen a real transformation in children's abilities to develop their own questions that really can drive deep inquiries, and because they've written and developed those questions they tend to have a real personal resonance for them" (Lisa Cuthbertson-Novak, personal communication, 2016).

This student agency has the potential to create more meaningful learning locally and globally, and the active role of students increases student engagement. This new balance in decision making is inevitable because students are digitally connected to massive amounts of information and want to take an active, not passive, role in their learning. School leader Simon Trembath notes, "Our students now see themselves as really active participants in their learning. They're working with teachers collaboratively to decide where their learning journey takes them, how they share their learning and who they share their learning with" (personal communication, 2016).

online resources

The new partnerships are illustrated in Video 5.1, Learning Partners: Collaboration (available at **www.npdl.global**), created by our **New Zealand** cluster, where they describe the impact of the 6Cs on the relationship between teachers and students and students with students and the impact of collaborative practices.

Learning Partners: Collaboration

Kahukura Cluster; Christchurch, New Zealand

When we began, the teachers and students were at the lowest level of the collaboration progression, but this has completely reversed. As we embedded the student language in the daily work, our students could see where they were but also the pathway they needed to take to move forward. Our children are taking what they are learning about collaboration and using it to collaborate at circle time, conference time, in their writing, reading, and all other aspects of their work. We see that the work standard is rising and the ideas are deeper. Students are thinking more about what they are doing and what those around them are doing. A traditional Maori technique, Tuakana Teina, builds learning relationships between older and younger students. Teachers are observing older students developing deeper understanding and tolerance as a result of their role as peer-to-peer teachers.

Students describe the impact on their learning this way, "It's so much better because I don't have to listen to things I already know" and can articulate clearly not only where they are in their progress but also the pathway they need to take to get to better: "I love it because I've moved up in my literacy."

The following story from the **Netherlands** cluster captures the transformation in the relationship of teachers to their craft and to the students.

Unthinkable One Year Ago

Jelle Marchand and Annemarie Es; Netherlands

A very clear success, which 1 year ago was unthinkable, is the positive impact of partnerships between teachers and students, where we see a slow shift in the curriculum on behalf of the contribution from students. Teachers experience that co-creation with students and consciously thinking about the curriculum leads to motivated students, which makes teaching easier than the class frontal approach. Teachers are aware that the (Dutch teaching) methods alone will not achieve their goals. Teachers consciously design their lessons and increasingly demonstrate the use of the Inquiry Circle as a core part of their work. Teachers learn to develop the skills to set good goals and ask the right questions, and the Success Criteria are determined by teachers and students collectively. Researching and designing learning by teachers and students provides meaningful learning experiences. What we experience time and time again is that we give people back their professionalism. Participation in the partnership has resulted in a shift in mindset for many. Which is great! However, this transformation is not easy. Besides, we have no choice, and there is no turning back; the appreciation and satisfaction of the students makes the effort worth it. Students' motivation, commitment, and joy in learning have increased significantly.

Schools and districts that embrace the new roles and partnerships are seeing exponential growth in student engagement and success. Previously we shared the example from Uruguay, where students were co-designing the learning with the teacher. Their initial curiosity was essential in setting a new direction with robotics and then deepened as they began teaching other classmates how to use the new robotics approach and then later how to evaluate progress. As well we highlighted Glashan School in Ottawa, Canada, where students took responsibility as a Deep Learning Leadership Team for the evolution of deep learning within the school and connected it to questions of environmental stability in Sweden. Further afield in **Australia**, students led a three-school exhibition of students working to solve problems of the future.

Young Minds of the Future Expo

Ringwood North Public School, Canterbury Public School and Chatham Public School; Victoria, Australia

The Young Minds of the Future (YMF) exhibition was a student-led exhibition held on September 9th, 2016, at Canterbury Primary School. This was the culmination of a truly collaborative learning experience for both students and teachers across three primary schools: Ringwood, Canterbury, and Chatham. This learning experience gave participants the opportunity to explore the concept of *future* and how the past has shaped our world and influences the years to come. Students brainstormed different areas of interest such as health, sport, education, gaming, food, and transport, and then compiled a list of questions they were curious about. Based on the list, teachers created a series of tutorials planned using iTunes U. Students signed up to attend the tutorials they were interested in. Students learned about augmented and virtual reality, child app developers, technological advances in sports, different modes of transport and their impact on the environment, sustainable fashion trends, and more.

Working in teams, students chose an area to focus on and were required to predict what the future of their chosen field would look like based on findings from tutorials attended as well as their individual research. Predictions were to be shared at the YMF exhibition. Students worked through a keynote to document and guide their learning and checked in regularly with their allocated teacher. Working together, students came up with what their YMF exhibition would focus on, why this idea was important, what research supported their claims, what their stall would look like, and how they would engage and interact with their audience on the day.

The exhibition was promoted and advertised by students, inviting members of the local community to attend. To learn more, view Video 5.2, Young Minds of the Future, at **www.npdl.global**.

online resources

In these examples and others we are seeing that students are equal partners and co-constructors of the learning impacting their schools and communities. This increases student engagement, and this new role for students pushes on the traditional role of teachers. For students to become equal partners, teachers' roles must also change toward becoming activators, coaches, and catalysts.

A New Role for Teachers

Learning is complex, and students are multidimensional. In deep learning, teachers are using their professional knowledge and expertise to engage and support learning in new and different ways with new relationships and ways of interacting emerging. As students begin to master the learning process, the teacher's role shifts gradually away from explicit structuring of learning tasks and toward more explicit feedback that activates the next learning challenge. There is no one way to engage in every situation, but let's take a look at three ways teachers can think about their role to engage and propel the learning process (see Figure 5.4).

Figure 5.4 • A New Role for Teachers

Activator	Culture Builder	Collaborator
Establish challenging learning goals, success criteria, and deep learning tasks that create and use knowledge	Establish norms of trust and risk taking that foster innovation and creativity	Connect meaningfully with students, family, and community
Access a repertoire of pedagogical practices to meet varying needs and contexts	Build on student interests and needs Engage student voice and agency as co-designers of the learning	Engage with colleagues in designing and assessing the process of deep learning using collaborative inquiry
Provide effective feedback to activate next level of learning	Cultivate learning environments that support students to persevere, to exercise self-control, and to feel they belong	Build and share knowledge of the new pedagogies and the ways they impact learning

Source: Copyright © 2017 by New Pedagogies for Deep Learning™ (NPDL)

Teacher as Activator

The term *activator* emerged from John Hattie's (2012) analysis of over 1,000 meta-studies worldwide into the impact of different teaching and learning strategies on student learning. His findings led him to distinguish two sets of strategies—one he labeled *facilitator* and one *activator*. While the facilitator set of strategies is more effective than the traditional "sage on the stage," Hattie (2012) found that the impact of the activator was three times greater than the facilitator with an effect size of .72. In other words, being a "guide on the side" is *too passive*. By contrast, the set of strategies associated with the activator role include teacher-student relationships, metacognition, teacher clarity, reciprocal teaching, and feedback. To that list we would add catalyst and coach since teachers as activators play a dynamic, interactive role with students to define meaningful learning goals, establish success criteria, and develop student skills in learning to learn so that they become reflective, metacognitive learners. Activators have a wide range of pedagogical capacities and use thinking tools and explicit questions to scaffold learning for that particular student or task so that students are challenged to meet the next level of learning and develop increasingly complex capacities and competencies. Other instructional frameworks that reinforce and support the activator role also fit here. For example, SOLO (Structure of the Observed Learning Outcome) allows teachers to classify outcomes regarding their complexity, enabling them to assess students' work regarding its quality (Biggs & Collis, 1982). Finally, teachers work in partnerships with students to make the students' thinking and questions about learning more visible. They use effective feedback processes and foster self- and peer feedback capacity in students to guide students to unleash their potential.

Teacher as Culture Builder

Cracking the black box of motivation is high on any teacher's list. Paul Tough (2016), in his book *Helping Students Succeed: What Works and Why*, combined research from several disciplines to look at how attitude and the learning environment can be good predictors of academic success for children, particularly those from disadvantaged backgrounds. He makes the point that research on motivation shows that messages about belonging, possibility, and skill shape motivation and have a huge effect on how willing and likely students are to want to work hard and push themselves.

Students who are advantaged arrive more ready to learn and often have parents with higher levels of education—their parents teach them the attitudes and skills required to persist in school, even in the face of challenges; they coach them in responding appropriately to classes that may not seem interesting or relevant. This provides huge social capital advantages.

Students who have historically done poorly in school have parents who love them but may not know how to help them, or given the requirements of multiple jobs, unemployment, stress, and so on, they may not have the time, skills, or resources to help. Traditional approaches to education for students in these circumstances can be toxic—boring, irrelevant, and a constant reminder of how inadequate they are. For these students to succeed, it is critically important that their teachers and the school help them set high personal expectations, learn how to manage their own learning, and be engaged in learning by involvement in real-world problem solving so that their learning experiences are connected to their world and culture. Their learning experiences must engage students and show them they are capable learners.

Tough (2016) proposes that these are not skills we teach in the traditional ways in schools but rather the product of the environment we are building that makes students able to persevere, to exercise self-control, to behave in all of the ways that are going to maximize their future opportunities. The challenge is how to create the environment that fosters these traits. Tough (2016) identifies three ideas that motivate kids: feelings of belonging, feelings of confidence, and feelings of autonomy—all intrinsic motivators.

Teachers then have a significant role to play in creating a culture that values and builds on the interests of students and gives them a sense of belonging

CHAPTER 5

and connectedness. Some teachers use morning meetings to build community and connection, establish norms, and shape culture. Others, as we saw in Glashan school, fostered student leadership as the key to implement deep learning in a middle school. Students took on roles as decision makers and doers so that student voice and agency were unleashed in the real work of shifting learning across the school. Finally, we are seeing that the nature of the deep learning tasks is intrinsically motivating for students because they delve into topics that are of real interest to them, have authentic meaning, and are more rigorous. It makes them want to persist and succeed. We are seeing that this combination of autonomy, belongingness, and meaningful work is building capacity in all students, but we have emerging evidence that it is catalytic for success in previously disadvantaged or underengaged students who are beginning to flourish.

Teacher as Collaborator

Teachers play a crucial role in engaging in learning partnerships with families, communities, and students. One of the emerging findings is that the co-design of learning by teachers and students that builds on student needs and interests and links to authentic learning significantly impacts engagement. Our caution here is that co-design is not an end in itself; rather it is a mechanism for developing student-teacher relationships that are based on knowing deeply student needs, strengths, and aspirations combined with honesty and respect. It would be possible to co-design a learning unit with students that is multidisciplinary and focused on a real-world problem in a superficial way—we have all seen countless units that purport to build understanding of world cultures or equity and amount to little more than celebrations of local foods and costumes or units on dinosaurs or recycling that are engaging but not deep. Quite often things that look "cool" are not deep with respect to learning. The crucial discriminator of deep learning is the depth of acquisition of the new competencies. The discriminator of meaningful co-design is when students are establishing goals for development that move them to increasingly complex levels of growth on the competencies. Principal Teresa Stone put it this way, "Teacher framed and student led" (personal communication, May 2017). This movement toward increasingly complex acquisition of the 6Cs must be the anchor that drives the learning design and what makes the learning deep.

Quite often things that look "cool" are not deep with respect to learning.

The second aspect of teacher as collaborator is deeper collaboration with professional colleagues. Teachers gravitate toward greater transparency as they collaborate to assess starting points, design learning experiences, and reflect on student progress. The common language and knowledge building about practices is a powerful catalyst for change and a vehicle for forging new relationships within grades and departments and across schools, regions, and globally. There is much that teachers can do for themselves to learn from each other, but there is also a role for school leaders in which they proactively enable focused collaboration.

A New Role for Leaders

Leaders in schools where deep learning thrives influence the culture and processes that support working and learning together in purposeful ways (Fullan, 2014; Fullan & Quinn, 2016). They operate as "lead learners," recognizing they cannot control results by intervening as the lead teacher inside every classroom but rather by orchestrating the work of teachers, students, peers, and families to be focused on collaboratively moving toward deep learning. Lead learners do this in three ways: by modeling learning themselves, shaping culture, and maximizing the focus on deep learning.

Modeling Learning

School leaders model being learners themselves by actively participating in tackling new approaches. They don't simply send teachers to workshops but learn alongside them, and this immersion in learning has the added benefit of building trust and relationships. Leaders then have a better understanding of what is needed to implement change. Lead learners know the attributes of effective capacity building and make it a priority with appropriate resources and support. Finally, they are attentive to intentionally developing teacher leaders and others to expand the work.

Shaping Culture

Lead learners cultivate deep collaborative work by establishing a nonjudgmental culture and conditions that build trust. They do that not only by participating as learners themselves but also by setting norms that it is good to take risks as long as there is learning from failures. They foster vertical and lateral relationships within and across schools by establishing collaborative learning structures to plan, examine student work products, and assess quality of learning designs. As well, they establish mechanisms for learning regularly from the innovative practices and using that knowledge to adjust next steps. In this work, school leaders, along with teachers, establish a climate of transparency, innovation, specificity of practice, and continuous improvement.

Maximizing the Focus on Deep Learning

Leaders keep the focus on a small set of goals to foster deep learning and identify success criteria. They build precision in pedagogy developing a set of highly impactful practices, ensuring they are understood by all and used consistently in the design and assessment of learning. The work of coaches, team leaders, and support personnel are coordinated to maximize impact and achieve deep learning. Deep collaborative practices such as collaborative inquiry and protocols for examining student work are resourced and used consistently. Deep learning leaders not only encourage and support innovation, but also help sort out what works best with respect to student engagement and learning.

A New Role for Families

We have long known that families play a vital role in students' success and even more so for students of poverty or disadvantage.

> Families are composed of individuals who are competent and capable, curious, and rich in experience. Families love their children and want the best for them. Families are experts on their children. They are the first and most powerful influence on children's learning, development, health, and wellbeing. Families bring diverse social, cultural, and linguistic perspectives. Families should feel that they belong, are valuable contributors to their children's learning, and deserve to be engaged in a meaningful way. (Ontario Ministry of Education, 2014c)

So how do schools and teachers engage families in meaningful ways? The key is to build a solid *partnership*. The ability of teachers and schools to work in partnership with families needs to go beyond two-way communication, parent-teacher conferences, and school events to invite participation of families in a range of roles. The seminal work of Joyce Epstein highlights the need for diverse ways to connect (Epstein, 2010; Epstein et al., 2009; Hutchins, Greenfeld, Epstein, Sanders, & Galindo, 2012). This is critical for all but especially for our children of poverty. Current research such as that of Paul Tough (2016) points out that extreme stress and childhood adversity hinders school success and that the best tool for compensating is the environment in which the child spends their time. Teachers and schools play a role, but it is only when they work in concert with families that we can hope to see real advances. The environmental factors that matter most have to do with the relationships they experience—the way the adults in their lives interact with them—particularly in times of stress. These interactions in early life provide cues to what the world is like and strengthen neural connections in the brain between regions that control cognition, emotion, language, and memory. When the adults can help children handle stressful moments, they impact the child's long-term ability to manage emotions.

Making headway on such a complex issue requires real partnership between schools and families based on mutual trust and transparency. This means a shift to joint power and decision making and a movement toward real-time communications and willingness to engage using the tools of the digital world. As we begin to partner with parents on the deep learning agenda, two things are happening. First, parents are excited by the increased engagement and depth of student learning, and second, they are eager to contribute to the learning experiences. Early strategies that show promise are the proliferation of student-led conferences and exhibitions of learning where students articulate what, how, and how well they are learning, and the use of blogs, Twitter, Instagram, and other digital tools to share student investigations and findings.

A New Role for Community

The boundaries between the classroom and the world are becoming blurred. More and more we see teachers and students reaching out to experts and connecting with schools and resources down the street or around the globe. This requires teachers to establish a wider network, develop skill in building relationships with those they may not know, make critical distinctions about what is worthwhile, and trust the innovation process. Simultaneously they must develop those same skills in their students. This means just-in-time scaffolding of learning, as a teacher of 14-year-olds in **Hamilton, Canada**, found recently.

"Just-in-Time" Learning

Grade Eight Teacher; Hamilton, Canada

The class took on the authentic task of getting a new creative playground designed and built for the school. The students formed departments and held weekly staff meetings to design and monitor the construction. One task included contacting local experts to develop the specifications for the bid. The students divided the task and contacted companies by e-mail. Several days passed, and not one response arrived. The teacher realized that he had assumed that since his students spent half their life on devices that they would be skilled at that form of communication. It became apparent that they needed skills in persuasive writing and crafting of key messages. Once students learned the basics of connecting and building a partnership, the project continued successfully, and community members who had not replied to the original e-mail became deeply engaged in the work.

Rich resources exist in local and global communities, but students and teachers must develop the explicit skills to connect and build those relationships. A second example from a rural school in **Southern Tasmania** highlights the changes for both students and the community that emerge when learning partnerships are the focus.

Partnerships for Change

Rural High School Students; Tasmania, Australia

School, business, and community connections are fundamental in building the capacity of our students to succeed into the future and make meaningful contributions to society. In 2013, Tasman District School saw a unique opportunity to be heavily involved in a partnership with the international construction company Lendlease and to strengthen ties with the local Tasman Peninsula community. Through Lendlease's global community and professional development program Springboard, the Tasman Peninsula—an hour and a half from Hobart in Tasmania—was identified as their next area for connecting with regional communities. The school and community were involved in consultations that identified different areas of need and potential across the region, including tourism, community leadership, volunteering, business class, and school infrastructure.

Students from Years Nine through Twelve (ages 14–18) chose an interest group and worked alongside community members and Springboard delegates. The community members and global delegates chose interest areas based on their skills. All Year Eight students participated in Business Class, an entrepreneurial group incorporating students, school staff, and Springboard delegates, which focused on three areas: sustainability, service, and enterprise.

The outcomes of these programs have been incredible: Students who were previously disengaged with schoolwork took the lead in developing ideas for community projects; students who would not engage with unfamiliar people now confidently presented in front of hundreds of people including CEOs and Department of Education delegates; and students who have had conflict in the past worked together to complete projects and raise money. The practical links with curriculum and being able to show understanding in a tangible way were great benefits, and now students are making links between school and industry. For some students to have an adult take an interest in them and what they want to do in the future builds the confidence they need to pursue their education.

Our students understand what true collaboration is and that their ideas can be taken seriously. An example of this is a group of boys who wanted to build a graffiti wall to practice on. With the support of the delegates, they wrote a proposal, presented, and costed it, and now have a graffiti wall that was constructed by community members, students, and Lendlease delegates. The students learned how to draw a scale plan from an architect and engineer, measure and assess the grounds, cost the project materials, place orders, and construct the wall over a series of sessions. This kind of opportunity only exists when business and industry get on board with schools. Another example has been a Tasman Peninsula activity book for kids, which was developed by the students from the school and community members and with input from the delegates as well. This project involved students liaising with many different environmental, tourism, and business groups to gain support and sponsorship. It involved the students and community members running classes to develop the activity pages throughout the book and then presenting the finished product to showcase their achievements to a wide range of stakeholders. These examples show just how important real collaborative partnerships are when there is equal involvement from community, business, and school.

These partnerships have provided the opportunity to be creative and collaborative in unfamiliar situations, think critically, and communicate ideas in challenging situations, and have developed students' character and their place as citizens of the world, but more important, brought that global perspective to the Tasman Peninsula.

Final Thoughts

The new learning partnerships we have just described are a distinctive feature of deep learning. New roles for students, teachers, leaders, families, and community are emerging. This transformation of roles requires shifts in control, decision making, engagement, and accountability. As such, it represents a radical change in the culture of traditional schooling. Accompanying this shift are the remaining three elements of the learning design: the learning environment, leveraging digital, and pedagogical practices that best foster deep learning. Together, the four elements of the learning design constitute the teaching conditions that are required for the 6Cs to flourish.

Notes

_____

_____

_____

_____

_____

_____

_____

_____

_____

_____

_____

_____

_____

_____

_____

_____

_____

_____

_____

❝ Education is not
preparation for life;
education is life itself. **❞**

—JOHN DEWEY

Chapter 6

DESIGNING DEEP LEARNING

Learning Environments, Leveraging Digital, Pedagogical Practices

Learning Design

Making the 6Cs come alive in classrooms is accelerated by using our four-fold solution—the learning design elements (Figure 6.1). In practice, the four elements of learning design are integrated and mutually reinforcing.

Figure 6.1 • **Four Elements of Learning Design**

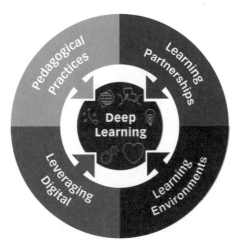

Source: Copyright © 2014 by New Pedagogies for Deep Learning™ (NPDL)

As we saw in Chapter 5, learning partnerships is one of four elements of learning design that are shifting rapidly and dramatically the way in which students, teachers, leaders, families, and communities are engaging in deep learning. In this chapter, we examine the remaining three elements—learning environments, leveraging digital, and pedagogical practices—and the way they work in concert with learning partnerships to foster deep learning experiences.

We begin with a recognition that deep learning will only flourish if we reimagine the ideal learning environment for today's learner.

Learning Environments

The second element of learning design is the learning environments depicted in Figure 6.2. This element considers a set of decisions that focus on creating "the modern learning 'space' which includes physical and virtual spaces but more importantly the cultural and relationship spaces" (Miller, 2017).

Researchers and practitioners from a wide range of disciplines—early childhood, psychology, cognitive science, school architecture, and design—maintain that the learning environment is the "third teacher" that can enhance the kind of learning that optimizes student potential to respond creatively and meaningfully to future challenges or detract from it (Fraser, 2012; Helm, Beneke, & Steinheimer, 2007; Ontario Ministry of Education, 2014b; OWP/P Cannon Design Inc., VS Furniture, & Bruce Mau Design, 2010). Two aspects of learning environment are essential and interrelated. The first involves the cultivation of a culture of learning to unleash the potential of adults and students alike, and the second addresses the design of physical and virtual space that optimizes the acquisition of the competencies.

Figure 6.2 • Learning Environments

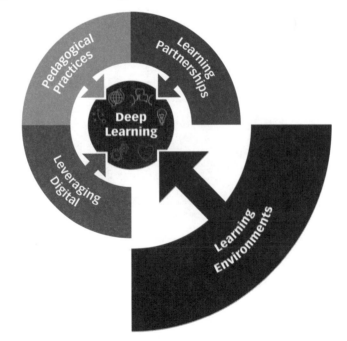

Source: Copyright © 2014 by New Pedagogies for Deep Learning™ (NPDL)

Cultures of Learning

How do we transform traditional classrooms to cultures of learning that cultivate energy, creativity, curiosity, imagination, and innovation? We discussed previously the importance of meeting students' basic need for autonomy, competence, and relatedness (Ryan & Deci, 2017) and the related finding that when teachers create an environment that promotes these feelings, students exhibit much higher levels of motivation. Teachers do this when they intentionally create norms of belonging where every voice matters, when they model empathy and deeply listen to student needs and interests, and when they structure tasks so that students feel competent as learners. Autonomy is cultivated when students have choice, and competence develops when they are challenged just a bit beyond their current abilities (Tough, 2016). Ryan and Deci (2017) conclude that as competence, autonomy, and relatedness are fostered, intrinsic motivation thrives, and while this is important for all students, it can play an even greater role in the experience of disadvantaged students. While there is no one recipe for creating classrooms that foster deep learning, we see some common characteristics in those moving toward deep learning.

Characteristics of Classrooms Moving Toward Deep Learning

1. *Students asking the questions.* They have skills and language to pursue inquiry and are not passively taking in the answers from teachers.

2. *Questions valued above answers.* The process of learning, discovering, and conveying is as important as the end result.

3. *Varied models for learning.* Selection of approaches is matched to student needs and interests. Students are supported to reach for the next challenge.

4. *Explicit connections to real-world application.* Learning designs are not left to chance but scaffolded and built on relevance and meaning.

5. *Collaboration.* Students possess skills to collaborate within the classroom and beyond.

6. *Assessment of learning that is embedded, transparent, and authentic.* Students define personal goals, monitor progress toward success criteria, and engage in feedback with peers and others. (Fullan & Quinn, 2016, p. 97)

Questions to ask during the design phase include: How will we develop norms of respect, collaboration, a trusting community, a sense of risk-taking, time for curiosity and creativity, and student voice and agency?

Physical and Virtual Environments

If we want our students to be curious, connected collaborators, we need to provide multidimensional spaces that offer flexibility for large and small group collaboration; quiet places for reflection and cognition; active areas for investigation, inquiry, communication, and documentation; and rich resources that are transparently accessible. Innovative learning environments are emerging across the globe. In Coachella Valley Unified, the district parked buses equipped with Wi-Fi in high poverty neighborhoods to increase digital access for students and families. In Derrimut Public School, the learning spaces are organized into *caves* for when students need to think deeply about something, *watering holes* when they need to share information and collaborate, and *campfires* for sharing the learning journey. We see rigorous, innovative learning in the most traditional of spaces—it just takes a bit of ingenuity and vision—while we see expensive new structures that lack a pedagogical approach to match the digital riches. To see innovative learning environments in action, view Video 6.1, Derrimut Public School, Australia, at **www.npdl.global**.

online resources

In these and countless other innovations it is not about the structures per se but the ways they are used to intentionally support the learning.

Making the walls of the classroom transparent is not just about redesigning space but requires taking stock of the ways we can connect inside and outside the classroom.

Making the walls of the classroom transparent is not just about redesigning space but requires taking stock of the ways we can connect inside and outside the classroom. If we want students to seek out experts in the community and beyond and to build knowledge from multiple fields, we need to identify ways to connect skills to discern appropriately and ways to build relationships in a diverse world. Our work has shown that when students are engaged they begin to connect both inside and outside the school and make learning a 24/7 proposition.

Learning environments are changing rapidly both culturally as new partnerships emerge and physically as the walls of learning become transparent. The exemplars featured at the end of this chapter illustrate the diverse and rich ways learning is connecting the world inside and outside the traditional classroom and with experts who may be across the country or world. One of the most powerful ways to make these new connections and open limitless possibilities is the third element of learning design—leveraging digital.

Leveraging Digital

The digital world is impacting every aspect of life, and schools are no exception. While devices have been on the scene in schools for decades, their potential has never been realized. We set forth here to describe the decision points that can be used to leverage digital so that it accelerates, facilitates, and deepens the learning process when used in tandem with the other three elements, as depicted in Figure 6.3.

Deep learning design needs to answer two questions:

a. How can digital be leveraged so that learning can be facilitated, amplified, and accelerated as student-driven learning is cultivated?

b. What transformative learning opportunities does digital provide that cannot be met with traditional approaches?

We use the term *leveraging digital* in place of *technology* to signal that we are not discussing devices, software, or apps of the day, but rather focusing on the role that interaction with digital can play in enhancing the learning. Effective use of digital facilitates deep learning partnerships with students, families, community members, and experts regardless of geographical location and supports student capacity to take control of their own learning both within and outside the classroom walls. While digital is an accelerator, it is the four elements of the new pedagogies together that are the drivers of deep learning outcomes. Our emphasis in NPDL has been not on the complexity of digital tools themselves but on how they can be leveraged in the direct development of deep learning.

Figure 6.3 • Leveraging Digital

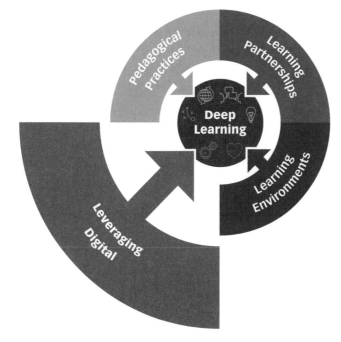

Source: Copyright © 2014 by New Pedagogies for Deep Learning™ (NPDL)

Access to knowledge is no longer confined to books or teachers but is ever evolving. In a recent trip to a used bookstore, one of us came across an Encyclopedia Britannica published in the '80s. It reminded us that we used to worry about teaching students research skills to go down the hall to the library and select from a relatively static set of resources. Fast forward to today and the teacher's role becomes one of ensuring students have the skills and competencies to discern, critically assess, discover, and create new knowledge using an almost limitless set of resources available online. Deep learning is focused on using digital ubiquitously as seamless parts of the learning rather than spotlighting the app or software of the week. In the past, we mostly asked students to solve problems that have already been solved. Today we have moved from asking our students to be consumers of knowledge to asking them to apply their solutions to real-world problems. The digital world gives us a mechanism to link to authentic audiences beyond the boundaries of schools and for doing that on a global scale.

This myriad of options creates crucial decision points for teachers to make about the thoughtful use of digital including media as an integral part of the learning. The range of options is accelerating daily, so we do not attempt to catalogue them here. Rather we recognize that in the learning design process, teachers need to select the most appropriate form of digital from the vast array of options and ensure that students have the skills to not simply use it but to be discriminating in how they use it to build knowledge, collaborate, or produce and share new learning. In practice, we are seeing this as an area where students are often taking the lead in both identifying and selecting the best uses of digital to enhance learning.

It is also the case that for developing countries and for students with special disabilities that adaptive technology can play an inexpensive and rapidly accelerating role in reaching tens of thousands of students operating in dispersed communities. To a certain extent, our Uruguay cluster represents a good example in this domain where the entire education system has made great gains in the last decade by leveraging digital.

The final element of learning design is pedagogical practices. Normally conceived in isolation—what are the best teaching practices available—our model requires that they be integrated as part and parcel of the foursome that constitutes the overall learning design.

Pedagogical Practices

During the process of determining what pedagogical practices will be most effective at attaining the learning goals and success criteria, teachers must consider the interplay between the four elements and how that feeds into the selection of pedagogical practices (see Figure 6.4).

Recall the snapshots of deep learning classrooms we saw in Uruguay, Finland, and Canada in Chapter 3, which conveyed a rich learning experience that extends beyond the classroom walls, engages students

Figure 6.4 • Pedagogical Practices

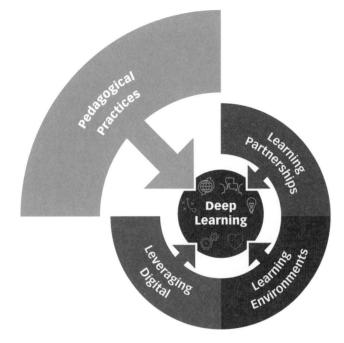

Source: Copyright © 2014 by New Pedagogies for Deep Learning™ (NPDL)

collaboratively, and ignites their passion. Teachers immediately recognize that fostering this new process of learning has implications for them as teachers and for every aspect of the teaching and learning process. In other words, inspiration and strong moral purpose—"I want my students to learn in this engaging way"—is not a strategy. Teachers also need to know how to begin to move from traditional lesson plans and pacing guides without jeopardizing student success. When we began talking with educators about NPDL, the first question from teachers was "Does this mean that what I was doing was wrong?" The answer is a resounding no. It's not about throwing out what we already know but putting a new lens of depth over many of the effective pedagogical practices from the past that are essential for deep learning and eliminating the outdated, ineffective ones. Beginning with a deficit mindset is never productive; rather, teachers need support to select the effective practices that should go forward and then learn how to infuse innovative approaches. Teachers must develop deep expertise in instructional and assessment practices if they are to maximize impact, leverage digital, and accelerate learning.

As we noted in the previous examples, we are seeing teachers who embrace deep learning beginning to think in terms of creating deep learning experiences and richer units of learning that provide time to develop the competencies and often utilize teaching models such as inquiry, problem-based, project-based, and multidisciplinary. These models most often require the teacher to take on the role of activator and for students to engage in choice and take responsibility for their learning. These longer learning experiences most often engage students in authentic, relevant problems or simulations where learning is applied. Most often this combination of choice, more meaningful tasks, and increased student responsibility leads to increased engagement—the first attribute suggesting a deeper learning process. So how do teachers get started?

Teachers don't need to start from scratch in selecting models but can draw from a rich history of deep learning approaches. Constructivism, student choice, and authentic learning are not new concepts; in fact, many educators have long advocated for an approach that puts the student at the center and provides meaningful, challenging opportunities to grow. Decades ago, Piaget (1966) introduced his four stages of cognitive development and the notion of learners building their own understanding. Seymour Pappert (1994) built on the concept of constructivism and also saw computers as a natural tool for problem-based learning to be used in an integral way that becomes seamless. Montessori (2013) and the Reggio Emilia approach are built on strong beliefs about early education and valuing the child as strong, capable, *and* resilient, rich with wonder, deep curiosity, and potential that drives their interest to understand their world and their place within it.

Teachers need to develop skills in drawing from a range of models to prepare students who will be lifelong learners. Learning is a continual process and now occurs in a variety of ways—through communities of practice, personal networks, and completion of work-related tasks. Use of technology is altering or rewiring our brains, and many of the processes previously handled by learning theories (especially in cognitive information processing) can now be off-loaded to, or supported by, technology. Models of learning are evolving, and teachers need an extensive repertoire of practices.

We describe the new pedagogical practices as a *fusion of the most effective pedagogical practices with emerging innovative practices that together foster the creation and application of new ideas and knowledge in real life.*

The graphic in Figure 6.5 provides a sampling of rich options for teachers to make selections in designing learning experiences. We describe the new pedagogical practices as a *fusion of the most effective pedagogical practices with emerging innovative practices that together foster the creation and application of new ideas and knowledge in real life.*

The global partnership operates as a living laboratory, and thus the graphic is in constant evolution as new practices are refined and shared collaboratively. In practice it means teachers are constantly honing a deep knowledge of learning and assessment processes. They need to know how to scaffold experiences and challenges, finely tuned to the needs and interests of students and maximized through relevance, authenticity, and real-world connections. Teachers need a wide repertoire of strategies to meet diverse student needs and interests and a deep understanding of proven models such as inquiry and problem-based learning. In addition to these foundational effective practices, teachers are developing expertise in innovative practices and uses of digital for both learning and assessment. Teachers are faced with a tsunami of choices. There is no one way to design deep learning, but the first step is to develop skill and knowledge of both foundational

Figure 6.5 • **Fusion of Effective Pedagogical and Emerging Innovative Practices**

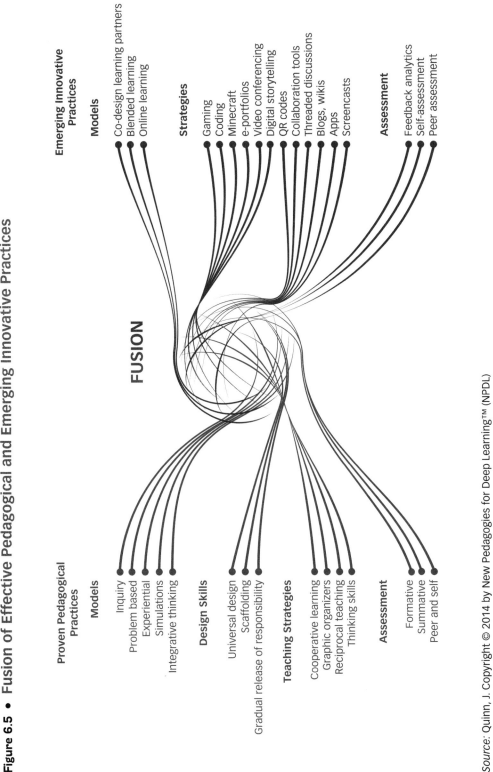

and innovative practices so that teachers can activate learning seamlessly as the learning experiences evolve. While this may sound daunting, we are finding that the explicitness combined with the transparency as teachers share their practices is making the learning and acquisition of new ways seamless and exponential.

Incidentally, in a playful moment we responded to our critics who observed that we had some nerve claiming that we were dealing only with *new* pedagogies. We readily acknowledge that there are new and old pedagogies and that both categories encompass good and bad practices (Fullan & Hargreaves, 2016). Hence the following fourfold figure in Figure 6.6.

Figure 6.6 • **Old and New Pedagogies**

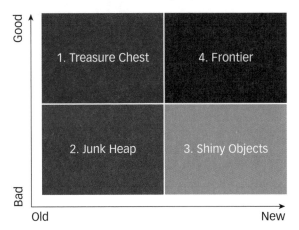

Source: Copyright © 2014 by New Pedagogies for Deep Learning™ (NPDL)

There are good old pedagogies (e.g., constructivism), bad old pedagogies (e.g., teacher talk), bad new pedagogies (e.g., aimless use of digital), and good new pedagogies (e.g., learning partnerships). Deep learning is about finding and developing the most powerful old and new pedagogies whether they be treasure troves from the past or on the frontier of learning.

Be that as it may, precision of pedagogical practices is an essential foundation for deep learning. Today bright spots of inquiry-based learning, problem-based learning, project-based learning, integrative thinking, knowledge building, and digital innovations can be found across schools and countries. An example of building on the inquiry model comes from Grovedale West Primary School in **Australia**.

> Deep learning is about finding and developing the most powerful old and new pedagogies whether they be treasure troves from the past or on the frontier of learning.

Kids in Australia Building a Mini Library for Kids in Malaysia

Grades One and Two; Grovedale West Public School, Victoria, Australia

The school has focused deeply on literacy for a number of years and used the inquiry process. In Grades One and Two, a young boy dreamed of building a mini library for the Malaysian community he was returning to, because he noted that there were not many books available in that community and that they were very expensive. Teachers designed a long-term project to bring his dream to life. They designed learning experiences for the students that helped them collect books, write persuasive letters to publishers, design and write their own stories, and organize fund-raisers to help pay for the shipping of over 600 books to Kuala Lumpur. My Mini Library has now been set up in Kuala Lumpur, and negotiations are underway with the Malaysian education authorities to create a mobile library that can take the books out to children in the suburbs of the capital city. The impact did not stop there because the school has been shortlisted for the Order of Australia Association's Citizenship Awards based on this project.

In Video 6.2, Mini Library in Malaysia: Grovedale West Primary School (available at **www.npdl.global**), you can see how Grovedale West students are able to articulate how their actions have made a difference to their lives and the lives of others and the process teachers used to foster the learning.

This learning experience was designed collaboratively across the school. Teachers utilized the inquiry model but blended it with specific literacy strategies, incorporated scaffolding so that all students could contribute, used enhanced cooperative learning approaches to build collaboration, and utilized digital to connect with experts, corporate partners, and the municipal leaders in Malaysia. Teachers were not able to make all the pedagogical decisions in advance, but as the learning goal became clearer, they could intentionally draw from a repertoire of shared pedagogical practices to tailor the learning experience. The impetus for this experience arose from the interest and voice of one student, but they were able to amplify that as the other voices of students sought to be part of the endeavor.

This element of our model—pedagogical practices—is crucial in building a pathway for students to develop their competencies. As we just saw at Grovedale West, new pedagogical practices are fostering new relationships and ways of interacting because students take greater control of their own learning. The second element of learning design—*learning partnerships*—is evolving because teachers use their professional knowledge and expertise to engage with students, families, and community in new ways.

Making the Four Elements Gel

There is not one cookie-cutter approach to facilitating deep learning. The four elements combined with the 6Cs are helping thousands of teachers ask critical design questions and be more intentional in developing learning experiences that challenge and extend the learning to make it deep.

Our Australian cluster created a template (see Figure 6.7, also available at **www.npdl.global**) that serves as a visual organizer for design.

Figure 6.7 • Elements of Deep Learning Placemat Organizer

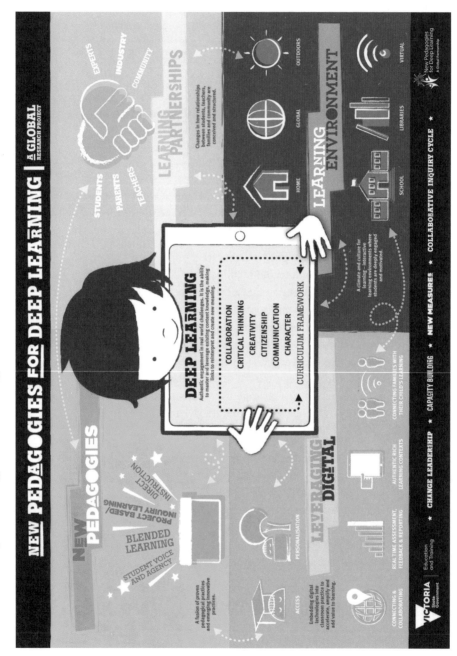

Source: State of Victoria (Department of Education and Training)

The use of the placemat organizer has spread across the seven countries as a way to consider all four elements of design and combine them visually. The natural global spread is a strong validation that teachers value a framework for their thinking.

Focusing on the four elements has grounded design efforts and provides a starting point for collaborative and individual planning. As noted by a cluster leader, "A strength has been being able to talk about and identify depth, look at how we've grown over a year, and say where we are on the continuum of the four quadrants of the new pedagogies framework. That's where we're building strength" (personal communication, July 2016). Clarity about the 6Cs combined with common language, understanding, and powerful pedagogies are helping teachers identify new pedagogies in action. This growing precision in outcomes and the learning process is establishing conditions for deep learning to take off on a massive scale.

Final Thoughts

Using the 6Cs and the four elements in learning design provides a powerful foundation for learning. Partnerships—Chapter 5—are a catalyst for much of our deep learning developments. While the lone learner can still be a viable option for some, and while all of us should have the capacity to learn on our own, in the end it is the combination of autonomy *and* collaboration that makes the learning world go round. Learning is a *social* phenomenon—increasingly so in the digitally connected world.

The other three elements—environment, digital, and pedagogy—make up the set. Moreover, all three are undergoing constant innovation. This means that deep learning itself must be dynamic. We think that we have a solid framework, and we see it as one capable of generating and absorbing change—adaptive if you like. Finally, our whole schema is based on the assumption that the learners "out there" are the main source of fuel for the future.

In the meantime, these learners are serving up deep innovation after deep innovation. We close off this chapter with six exemplars that show how some of our partners are incorporating the four elements and the 6Cs to create deep learning experiences.

What propels learning in all these examples are the collaborative processes that build capacity and accelerate the shift from current to future practices.

Call in the Clean-Up Buddies

"We're not just worrying about problems. We're doing things." Empowered words from an 8-year-old. He and his class participated in a yearlong outdoor interdisciplinary inquiry program. What started off as a short stream study project evolved into a yearlong call to action.

"A great way to show kids how to be involved in your community and how to initiate change. Shows them by empowering them that they are not 'just kids' they are members of our community and have a voice." (Parent)

"The kids were able to really see how their actions can bring real change to the town and environment. These skills will lead them to be stronger and more conscientious adults." (Parent)

Here's what happened: While students were conducting their stream study, they noticed garbage on the trail and decided to do something about it. So they teamed up with their Grade One friends and cleaned up the litter. They all returned to school, created sculptures with the plastic bottles, and presented their concerns to the school assembly. But they weren't done yet. They needed to better understand what motivates people to litter. So they created a survey and hit the streets to learn from community members. But they weren't done yet. Jen Wroe, their teacher, introduced them to Google Hangouts, documentaries, and online biologists and researchers. She continues, "They discovered how to input their garbage data collection to the Litterati Website . . . then decided to apply for funding from Learning for a Sustainable Future to fund a sign on the Millennium Trail to educate users. Students wrote the funding proposal themselves."

Next, they decided to present their concerns to the Parks and Recreation department of their municipality. Each student prepared a slide of information. That's when the mayor heard about these kids. He invited them to present to town council and initiate a media campaign. The students then hooked up with a local Grade Eleven media class and designed posters for town council. And by then, it was June.

Deep learning is a forever process and, as these Grade Three students demonstrated, can make a real difference in the world.

Grade Three   *Source:* Jen Wroe at Queen Elizabeth PS, Renfrew County

Failure Is Where Learning Begins

Teacher Andrew Bradshaw had an interesting problem. His Grade Twelve engineering students were consumed by achievement at the expense of their own learning; they were chasing grades rather than embracing creativity and deeper understanding. Bradshaw says, "Creativity in the engineering process is an often overlooked. . . . There is a real danger for engineering students to abandon their creativity in the pursuit of 'safe' and proven methods of obtaining good grades and 'winning' products."

So for 2 short weeks, Bradshaw posed a challenge for students that focused on creativity, character, and critical thinking: They had to apply their technical expertise as well as their innovative minds to develop a new solution to a $10 Sumo Bot. Students would design, source, build, and program a digital sumo bot, then compete against each other.

Bradshaw introduced students to creative thinking theory, and then together they set out success criteria that included taking risks, frugal resourcing, building rationale, and reflecting on the learning. Students learned to manage their time and built prototypes, while Bradshaw guided them on the side. A community-based engineering partner also came in a few times to work with the students.

Bradshaw explains, "Without exception, all students liked the project. . . . They liked converting junk into functional components. They liked the freedom of designing at will rather than being limited to what I provide in class. I like this aspect of it too."

As well, students learned to be creative with time and resource constraints—a real-world problem engineers encounter. Perhaps the most illuminating reflection comes from Erika, a student, "This challenge was a great opportunity for creative people to thrive, but also a terrifying experience for non-creative people." Normalizing risk and failure is a key part of the learning process. Failure is where learning begins.

Source: Andrew Bradshaw at Stratford Central SS, Avon-Maitland

> "Failure should not be the end. It should be the beginning of the learning." (Student)

> "This challenge was a great opportunity for creative people to thrive, but also a terrifying experience for noncreative people." (Student)

Grade Twelve
Computer Engineering

Curiosity Is Instinctive

Two teachers set out to try a new approach to teaching biology and literacy skills with their 12-year-old students. With a forest next door to the school, they assigned the students the following task: to adopt a small area of the woods and study it closely over time by taking notes, photographs, and measurements. Students were asked to keep a digital diary of what they were observing.

> **"Lessons were carried out without teacher interference. I only gave advice and motivated students."** (Teacher)

Technology was a natural for this outdoor learning task. Students used two-in-one Surface devices to capture the information they were collecting and interviewed external experts using Skype. They generated new knowledge and learning artifacts and used OneNote and Sway to convey the learning.

> **Curiosity is instinctive. Deep learning is natural.**

And the insights that emerged could not come from a textbook. By carving out their own little space in the woods and studying it over time, students began to notice the microwonders that live there—the trees, insects, soils, flora and fauna, the changes in seasons, and the effects of climate change. They were learning how to see a familiar forest with new eyes and feel a greater appreciation for the fragile species that inhabit it. And through that experience, students acquired competencies in character, citizenship, and critical thinking.

The students weren't the only ones surprised by what they observed. The teachers noticed that when they released responsibility to the students and provided them with choices, students thrived. As one teacher said, "It was enjoyable to watch the children work self-reliantly and enthusiastically." Curiosity is instinctive. Deep learning is natural.

Grade 7   *Source:* Moison Koulu and Tommi Rantanen in Turku

Take a Load Off

We all know about teacher workload.
And sometimes that workload is literal.
Every day teachers juggle with iPads, books,
and materials as they move from class to class or
from their car to the building. At Sacred Heart School, teachers put
this nuisance to students' innovative minds and challenged them to
collaboratively create a wheeled invention that could manage their
stuff more efficiently.

To begin, the teachers created a humorous video clip to situate the
problem and invite students into the design challenge. Then a "bring
your own wheels" day followed, immersing students into the theory
and practice of how wheels work. Students investigated propulsion
systems, energy transfer, and rubber band mechanisms. They also
participated in a QR code hunt to learn more about transporting loads
safely.

The students worked in collaborative, mixed age and ability groups
to design their solutions. They focused on critically analyzing each
other's ideas and plans. Parents, too, were engaged as partners,
digging up gently used materials like old prams and wheel belts
for students to use. Together students and parents built and tested
prototypes. Students presented their final inventions to the teachers,
explaining their thinking behind their inventions and their reflections
about the learning process.

Authentic design challenges are all around us. And when students
are given an opportunity to solve a real problem, it can not only be
motivating and resonating for students, but also take a real load off
teachers.

Source: Olivia Currie and Kath Clark at Sacred Heart

"The challenge the
teachers set for
the children was an
amazing learning
experience—my
son came home
and shared the
most he ever had
with us." (Parent)

"We flipped it
and students
taught us how
their inventions
worked." (Teacher)

Grades Three to Five

Rethinking
Giving

Who doesn't love a pajama day?
The Waimea Heights Primary School community had been enjoying pajama days for years, so much so that it just became part of the school culture. Somewhere along the way, they had lost sight of why everyone came to school in fuzzy slippers. Teachers wondered whether students really were aware of other needs in the world and why giving was important.

"It's a real life issue and not a work sheet." (Student)

"It has shown us that there are people out there who have to work extra hard just to do what we do every day." (Student)

So the students tried to better understand poverty—its causes, its ubiquity, and some solutions. Using digital technologies and connecting to partners, the students learned about microfinancing and crowd sourcing and how these small loans changed lives. By raising as little as $25, the students could be empowered to loan money to business start-ups anywhere in the world, and their loan would be returned to fund new loans, donate, or withdraw the money.

That motivated students to get busy on their own plans to raise $25 or more. The plans had to show originality, cost effectiveness, and independence. One group chose to make and sell homemade jellies in the community. Another student set up a donation box in a local hospital; she created the slogan, "Make a change with your change." Another group grew sunflowers from seeds and sold them. Once the fundraising projects were launched, the students researched the microloan requests and made informed decisions about where to channel the dollars they had collected. One student reflected on this learning, "It is good for us to know how it feels to lend money to those who barely have enough money to buy food and clean water. It also requires students to come up with their own ideas and plans. To get a result, the students must also be able to carry out plans they have created."

This deep learning strategy gave everyone pause to reflect. As one teacher remarked, "We're rethinking how we give."

Source: Pip Banks-Smith, Philippa Clymo, Peter Illingworth, Lynne Murray, and Emily Roberts at Waimea Heights Primary

Years Five and Six

Chocolate Can Be Bitter

At Livingstone Primary School, students learned that world economics isn't always sweet. Through simulations, online research, class discussions, and visits from guest speakers like Oxfam, students explored the issue of fair trade and free trade practices and their impact on workers within the chocolate industry. When the kids uncovered the harsh reality, they chose to take action.

They decided to thoroughly research organizations of their choice then follow up with letters—and they didn't mince words. One student levelled this remark, "We are astounded that your widely renowned business is not following Fair Trade practice." Another exclaimed, "I was horrified by how many horrible things were done to people who lived in Bangladesh and Africa. This must stop!" And another railed, "You stock merely eleven fair trade items, which is positively pathetic!" Such passion from 12-year-olds! But what are they learning?

In their reflections, students shared how an authentic task like this one amped up their overall engagement and also their skills in communicating and critical thinking. One student said, "Using SOLO maps has been helpful for me as it helped show me where I was missing information. . . . It was challenging for me to think of how to word my letter, but eventually I had it written in a way I was happy with." Another student reflected, "Another thing I found challenging was finding reliable websites because all chocolate brand websites wanted to make a good impression saying they had goals to become fair trade though they weren't doing too well." Other students valued the support from peers and acknowledged how collaboration supports the learning process.

Who knew chocolate could promote the 6Cs—citizenship, character, communication, critical thinking, creativity, collaboration—in the deep learning classroom?

Source: Jessica Morgan, Alee Cole, Caleb Webb, Jessica Burke, Zahara Forte, Alicia Wallwork, Claire McCubbin, and Ryan Forte at Livingstone Primary

"I was horrified by how many horrible things were done to people who lived in Bangladesh and Africa. This must stop!" (Student)

"Important partners of my learning were my peers. . . . They made me think deeper into arguments which helped us when we wrote the Fair Trade letter." (Student)

Years Five and Six

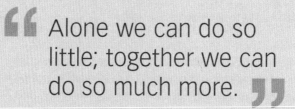

Alone we can do so little; together we can do so much more.

—HELEN KELLER

Chapter 7

COLLABORATION COUNTS
Inquiry That Shifts Practice

Cultivating Collaboration and Capacity

Of all the conditions that fuel deep learning, collaboration is at the heart of them. It is not collaboration as an end in itself (people can collaborate to do nothing or to do the wrong thing). Because deep learning involves innovation, and highly focused and specific new practices, it requires means for developing and accessing good ideas. If teachers are to make a rapid shift to using the new pedagogies, they need support from working with others to identify effective practices in their repertoire and to push new thinking and innovative practices. In a recent study of deeper learning in high schools, Jal Mehta (2016) noted,

> With all the talk of 21st-century skills and deeper learning, you might think that we have moved into an era where doing this kind of teaching and learning was the rule and not the exception. That couldn't be further from the truth. We can hope someday that we move to a world in which the larger systems are organized to incentivize and support deep learning, but we are not living in that world today. This means that teaching in the ways that promote deeper learning for all students is a subversive and countercultural act.

While there will always be the teacher outliers, the pioneers who are able to transcend the system and create pockets of excellence, we are interested in how to help large numbers of teachers, ultimately all teachers in a school, district, or jurisdiction, take on the new pedagogies that foster deep learning. We cannot rely on individual teachers to turn the tide one by one, but rather need an approach that mobilizes whole schools, districts, and systems to rethink their practice and provides models for that reflection and action planning.

We cannot rely on individual teachers to turn the tide one by one, but rather need an approach that mobilizes whole schools, districts, and systems.

Schools that are on the move toward building precision in deep learning begin by cultivating a ***culture of learning*** for both the educators and the students. If the teachers and leaders are not thinking deeply, it's unlikely they will create those conditions for their students. The schools and districts that are cultivating cultures of learning and moving most quickly with the new pedagogies build capacity using a range of strategies.

Strategies for Cultivating a Culture of Learning

- Establish norms and relationships that foster transparency of practice

- Build common language and skills in using a research-based instructional repertoire

- Create intentional mechanisms for identifying and sharing innovative practices

- Provide sustained opportunities for teachers to build their capacity—knowledge and skills—in using the new practices with feedback and support

What Is Capacity Building?

We started using the term *capacity building* over a decade ago to illustrate that much more than professional learning was required to make substantive long-lasting change in classrooms, schools, and systems. *Capacity* refers to the skills and competencies that individuals and groups must acquire to accomplish something of value. Thus mobilizing and sustaining whole system change consists of

> *collective capacity*, which we define as the increased ability of educators at all levels of the system to make the changes needed to improve results; and

> *capacity building,* which is defined as the process of developing the knowledge, skills, and commitment of individuals and organizations to achieve improved results.

Capacity building is still a broad term, so it is essential that schools and districts assess starting points and then identify precisely the content for their capacity building efforts. The four components of the *coherence framework* can provide an organizer for identifying the sets of skills and knowledge that must be developed in any organization focused on continuous improvement and innovation.

Transforming the learning-teaching process requires a sustained, multidimensional approach to capacity building that cultivates a culture of learning while fostering the acquisition and practice of new skills, knowledge, and attitudes. In our deep learning work, capacity building opportunities are fostered at all levels—classroom, school, district/cluster, and globally—and include

- Developing a shared knowledge and understanding of a set of tools and processes to design and measure deep learning

- Institutes that are multiday sessions with immersion in aspects of deep learning, and global deep learning labs that bring together practitioners and experts regionally and globally to share their expertise and build new knowledge

- Resources and exemplars of deep learning experiences created by teachers that are hosted on the deep learning hub that is a communication, collaboration, and data collection platform

The diversity of access and range of supports are designed to meet the varied needs. A key feature of all approaches is to amplify and accelerate the learning of new practices by leveraging collaborative learning. In previous chapters, we outlined the global competencies that are the heart of deep learning and described the four elements that foster their development. This chapter zeros in on one powerful process, *collaborative inquiry*, which is part of our comprehensive capacity building approach to deep learning. Collaborative inquiry helps teachers, schools, and districts to examine current models, practices, and assumptions for learning and to design systems that create the conditions that will support deep learning to flourish. While this process is used at every level of the New Pedagogies for Deep Learning (NPDL), we focus in this chapter on the powerful role it plays in enhancing the learning design and assessment process in schools and classrooms, as depicted in Figure 7.1.

Figure 7.1 • Collaborative Inquiry Supporting Learning Design

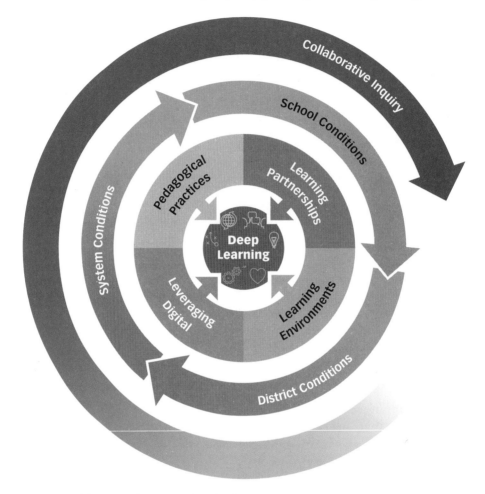

Source: Copyright © 2014 by New Pedagogies for Deep Learning™ (NPDL)

The Collaborative Inquiry Process

What is collaborative inquiry, and why is it important?

Collaborative inquiry is a process that explores the professional won-
derings and questions of educators by examining existing practices and
assumptions through engagement with colleagues. This process has
gained prominence as a powerful strategy for change because it simultaneously promotes professional learning and contributes directly to improved
student learning (Comber, 2013; Ontario Ministry of Education, 2014b;
Timperley, 2011). Collaborative inquiry is not only a method for problem solving and refining individual practices but also a system approach
for using evidence of student learning to build collaborative school
teams and generate shared professional knowledge that can be applied.
Finally, while students and student work are the focus of collaborative

inquiry, increasingly we are seeing students playing a role in the process as partners. Students are beginning to participate in identifying areas of inquiry, capturing evidence of their learning, and assessing that learning. Students become experts of their own learning experience. Collaborative inquiry is thus a powerful and practical form of capacity building that gives adults a deep learning model and experience that mirrors what we are hoping they will do with students. Engaging in this process creates a stance of openness to new learning and enables educators to work together to focus their professional learning.

NPDL supports teachers and students in a continuous process of collaboration in shaping deep learning experiences, as well as providing a method to assess the progress of learning and inform future learning experiences.

The modified collaborative inquiry process depicted in Figure 7.2 has four simple phases (adapted from the Deming Institute, n.d.).

Figure 7.2 • Collaborative Inquiry Process

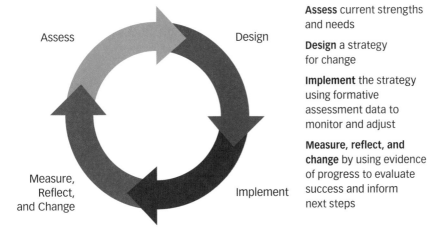

Assess current strengths and needs

Design a strategy for change

Implement the strategy using formative assessment data to monitor and adjust

Measure, reflect, and change by using evidence of progress to evaluate success and inform next steps

Source: New Pedagogies for Deep Learning™ (NPDL). Retrieved from www.npdl.global/Deep Learning Hub.

We examine next two ways this modified collaborative inquiry process is supporting a significant shift of practices in our NPDL partnership:

1. *Learning Design*—collaborative design of learning experiences; and

2. *Moderation*—a collaborative process of assessing student growth and assessing the quality of the learning designs to foster deep learning.

Collaborative Learning Design

Getting started in deep learning design accelerates when teachers collaborate within and across schools and when they have protocols, examples, and a process for working together. Connecting face to face or virtually with those who share your goals helps with problem solving the challenges and with committing to stick with new behaviors. This common focus on deep learning and the intentional sharing of practices leads to collective cognition and a realization by teachers that they are not working in isolation.

The collaborative process to design deep learning experiences uses the four phases.

Designing Deep Learning Experiences Collaboratively

Phase I: Assess

The first phase begins with assessing where students are, considering the curriculum expectations, and building on student interests to establish learning goals and success criteria. *Learning goals* are established based on an assessment of student needs, strengths, and interests as well as proficiency in the six global competencies. *Success Criteria* are identified to describe the evidence that would document that the learning goal has been achieved. Mixed method assessment is used to assess the degree of understanding and skill development.

Phase II: Design

The second phase involves designing learning experiences that engage students in acquiring the competencies to meet the learning goals and success criteria. This step includes the selection of the most effective pedagogies, consideration of the learning partnerships needed, development of an environment that fosters a culture of learning, and use of digital that leverages learning. Working collaboratively on these learning designs increases innovation because teachers are stimulated by the ideas of other teachers and the students themselves. While time consuming initially, teachers find that the protocols help them focus their energies, and after the first few designs, they can build on each other's expertise, are more innovative, and actually save time as they share the design workload.

Phase III: Implement

During the learning experience, the teacher monitors the learning, scaffolding as needed, asking questions, and guiding deeper discoveries by asking questions such as: " How well are the students learning?" "What evidence do I/we have of the learning?" "What do students need next to deepen their learning?" During this phase, teachers may observe in each other's class or share responsibility for students by grouping across classes for specific tasks or interests. Students develop skills in both peer and self-assessment. Students may even begin to lead the learning. As one teacher put it, "I used to think it was scary to let the students lead the learning, and now I think that it is one of the most valuable ways to create authentic learning for students as it allows them to take ownership and develop new ways to learn, express, share, and create their thoughts and ideas."

Phase IV: Measure, Reflect, Change

In the final phase of the process, teachers collaborate to document student learning. They consider a broad range of formal and informal assessment evidence from student work products and performances to measure growth in both academic content and competencies to inform their decisions. Student data then feeds into the next cycle of learning and provides rich input for the next learning design.

Skilled users of collaborative inquiry describe this process as a way of thinking about the work rather than being separate from the normal work. Sharing the learning designs across grade teams, departments, schools, and even globally provides vivid and powerful glimpses of what may be possible. Teachers view these *exemplars of learning experiences* not as something to be replicated but as a catalyst for thinking about how to deepen the learning of their own students.

One exciting evolution of the global partnership has been the development of global challenges. A global challenge poses a problem or inquiry that is of interest to a wide range of learners and invites teachers and schools from countries to participate. Students create products or outcomes over the same period of time. They use digital platforms for idea generation and iteration. The creative process of solving a common challenge, while taking into account different country perspectives and contexts, triggers meaningful dialogue, deepens knowledge, and fosters critical thinking. View the design prompt for a recent Deep Learning Task: UN Rights of the Child, in Figure 7.3.

Students and teachers across the globe took up the challenge and then shared their work on Twitter during a Deep Learning Lab held for 400 teachers and leaders in May 2017. This connectivity of teachers, leaders, and students is impressive. We are seeing that the language of deep learning has crossed country borders so that students and teachers can come together virtually or face to face and have highly impactful conversations of depth. There is a positive contagion that is helping the ideas spread like wildfire. On the next few pages, following Figure 7.3, we have captured a few of the student products that were posted as tweets to give you a glimpse of the passion for humanity that emerged.

Figure 7.3 • Global Challenge: UN Rights of the Child, Canada

Global Deep Learning Task: UN Rights of the Child
#NPDLchildrights

Task Goal and Description:
You and your learners are invited to participate in a Global Deep Learning Task while members of your country's/district's leadership team are attending the Deep Learning Lab in Toronto, May 1 to May 3. Learners and conference attendees will have the opportunity to be part of an online collaborative conversation on a topic of global relevance to students.

> **Big Idea:** We live in a complex, interconnected, and ever-changing global community that we hope to be governed by the inalienable 'Rights of the Child,' as set out by The United Nations.
>
> **PROMPT FOR LEARNERS/STUDENTS:**
> Based on your own knowledge and experiences, choose a right (or rights) which you believe to be the most critical for the safety, growth and development of youth around the world. Be prepared to share your understanding of that right and your action plan to ensure that right is recognized and supported in your town/city/nation or in a global context.

Platform:
The Global NPDL Twitter Chat will begin May 1st at 8:00am (EST-Toronto) and last for 3 days to accommodate the time changes of the participating countries. Participants will post using Twitter #NPDLchildrights. Tweets may include, but are not limited to links to student videos, websites, blog posts, plans, artefacts, art work, discussions, etc.

Instructions to Educators/Learners/Students:
Before (Prior to May 1):
- Educators should review the following documents, as appropriate, with learners prior to the start of the Twitter Chat:
    - https://www.unicef.org/rightsite/files/uncrcchilldfriendlylanguage.pdf
    - http://www.youthforhumanrights.org
    - **Link to Picture Book/Graphic:** https://www.unicef.org/rightsite/files/rightsforeverychild.pdf
    - https://www.unicef.org/rightsite/files/Frindererklarfr(1).pdf **(Child-friendly French)**
- Learners are to pursue an understanding of, and create an action plan for, the UN Right of the Child that is most accessible/relevant/suitable to them.
- Learners are to create a possibile action plan to share in a live Twitter chat during the Deep Learning Lab by using the #NPDLchildrights. Tweets may include, but are not limited to links to student video websites, blog posts, plans, artefacts, art work, discussions, etc.

During (May 1 to May 3):
- AMDSB NPDL Leads will moderate the live Twitter conversation with NPDL learners from clusters around the globe where learners will share and discuss their ideas and action plans with each other using the #NPDLchildrights.
- During the live Twitter chat participants are encouraged to question, challenge, and celebrate each other's contributions and learning by responding to Twitter #NPDLchildrights.
- Attendees of the Deep Learning Lab in Toronto will be encouraged to contribute to the live Twitter conversation as it unfolds using #NPDLchildrights.
- Big Ideas/Connected Themes will be projected at the Deep Learning Lab.
- Participants are encouraged include their country, school, and grade in an initial tweet.

After the Deep Learning Lab in Toronto:

- After the conversation, participants will be encouraged to complete at least one action on their plan and to continue collaborating with other learners in an ongoing Twitter chat from around the world using #NPDLchildrights.

NPDL Progression/Dimension Connections:

Critical Thinking	Communication	Collaboration	Creativity	Character	Citizenship
Collaborative Knowledge construction	Leveraging Digital	Social, emotional, and intercultural skills	Considering and pursuing novel ideas and solutions	Self-regulation and responsibility for learning	Solving ambiguous and complex problems in the real world to benefit citizens

Pedagogical Practices	**Learning Environment**
☐ Task is designed based on the interest and needs of all students ☐ Learning is personalized ☐ Student choice is embedded in the task ☐ Collaboration opportunities are continuous ☐ Task is authentic (based on real problems, real questions) ☐ Innovative strategies that leverage digital ☐ Clear learning goals ☐ Clear success criteria	☐ Task incorporates student voice ☐ Task requires purposeful learning partnerships ☐ Task accounts for the interests and needs of all students ☐ Learning is interactive ☐ Learning environment is authentic ☐ Learning environment includes virtual component
Learning Partnerships	**Leveraging Digital**
☐ Task requires purposeful learning partnerships ☐ Task ensures equity among partners ☐ Clear, transparent learning goals for all partners ☐ Clear, transparent success criteria for all partners	☐ Digital enables efficient and meaningful collaboration ☐ Digital is used to share new knowledge ☐ Task requires the use of digital

Source: Designed by Avon Maitland School District, Ontario, Canada (April 2017). Thanks to the staff of the Avon Maitland District School Board.

Two students made this sketchnote for #npdlchildrights on a ceiling tile for child labor.

An infographic advocating children's right to join clubs and make friends with other children. #npdlchildrights

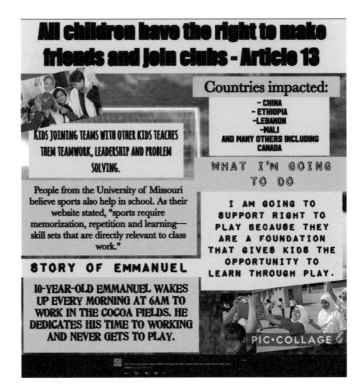

My action plan is that I will contact my MP (member of parliament) to help keep kids safe from kidnapping.

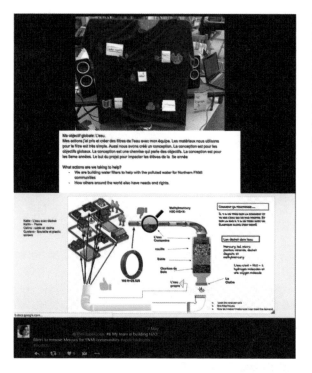

My team is building H$_2$O filters to remove mercury for FNMI (First Nations Metis Inuit) communities. #npdlchildrights @ocdsb @TheGlobalGoals

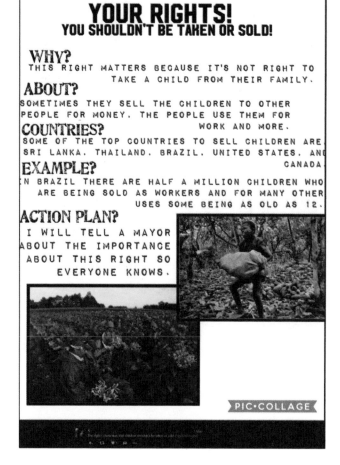

Students shouldn't be taken from their families. #npdlchildrights

Madison and Miranda, you have the right to a name. You have a right to a nationality. #npdlchildrights @scdsb

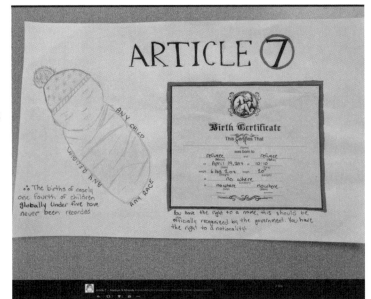

It is the right of every child to have an identity #npdlchildrights #kirkkonummi #veikkolankoulu at Kirkkonummi, Suomi.

Teachers and students use the deep learning competencies to anchor the design of deep learning experiences such as this global challenge. Teachers then share the learning designs and student work samples in what we call *exemplars*. These examples demonstrate the richness that evolves as the common language and understanding guides the work and serves as a catalyst for creating even more deep learning. The four elements of learning design examined in Chapters 5 and 6 guide teachers to create environments that use new partnerships, pedagogies, and digital to accelerate and amplify learning. The next stage of inquiry is to collaboratively look at the results of the learning designs and make decisions for subsequent steps during the moderation process.

Collaborative Assessment

The fourth phase of the collaborative inquiry process—*measure, reflect, change*—can be very powerful, and yet it is often the most neglected in day-to-day practice. Time to collaborate is scarce; it is more expedient to assign grades than look deeply into the quality of learning; and meaningful professional dialogue takes skill and knowledge. However, we have seen that the process of collaborative assessment (what we call *moderation*) of student work products and performances results in a deeper understanding of what the students have learned and builds professional reliability and validity for a more consistent determination of progress. The power of the process lies in the professional discussion about the learning and the sharing of effective strategies in preparing for the next stage of learning. This professional discussion generates new knowledge and is a catalyst for refining practice. In short, moderation is a strategy to examine and improve pedagogical practice.

In NPDL, we have used the process of moderation to engage teachers, other school leaders, and NPDL leadership teams at all levels of the partnership in professional dialogue centered on deep learning design, implementation, measurement, and outcomes. After teachers have designed, implemented, assessed, and reflected on a chosen deep learning experience, they have the opportunity to assemble and share examples. *Deep Learning Exemplars* are the examples of learning design, implementation, assessment, and outcomes that describe how deep learning develops and what it looks like in action. The intention is to develop a shared language and understanding around deep learning—its design, outcomes, and the new pedagogies that most effectively develop the 6Cs for all learners. The process provides teachers and leaders with examples of deep learning that can be leveraged in their own local contexts.

Moderation occurs at three levels:

- **School**—After teachers have shared their Deep Learning Exemplars with one another, participants engage in professional dialogue (moderation) to discuss the degree to which exemplars demonstrate and foster deep learning.

The power of the process lies in the professional discussion about the learning and the sharing of effective strategies in preparing for the next stage of learning.

- **Cluster**—Once schools have selected their deepest examples and shared them with their cluster or district team, cluster and school leaders, along with teachers, engage in a similar moderation process to select the richest examples of deep learning experienced in their cluster or district. These exemplars are then submitted for moderation (further collaborative assessment) at the global level.

- **Global**—Global moderation consists of a multi-week process in which groups of country leaders and teachers engage in discussion around new pedagogies, deep learning, and review the submitted deep learning experiences. The process results in the selection and sharing of globally moderated Exemplars throughout NPDL and to the wider education community. We take up the global moderation in more detail in Chapter 9.

Let's Consider the Typical Process at a School

Creating a culture of trust and transparency is essential for moderation to thrive. Successful moderation requires strong protocols, skilled learning partnerships among teachers and leaders, and the development of a culture of learning. One way to build the culture of trust and transparency is to establish shared norms. The four norms below have helped NPDL schools initiate, support, and accelerate the use of collaborative inquiry and the moderation process.

Four Norms to Accelerate the Collaboration

1. Assume the teacher has provided his or her best thinking at the time.

2. Presume that all details of the task and the thinking behind it cannot be fully shared within this example.

3. Be slow to judge. Recognize that we cannot fully know all that occurred in the class before this task or what will happen after.

4. We all need to assume a learning stance.

Teachers select a deep learning experience that will be moderated (examined) by peers. They provide an outline of the learning goals, success criteria, competencies addressed, and the new pedagogies used. They may describe the learning design using the four elements to identify the pedagogical practices selected, the types of learning partnerships and how they were fostered, the learning environment that was utilized both inside and outside the classroom, as well as how they have leveraged digital to facilitate or amplify learning. They include samples of students work and the mixed methods they used to assess student progress during the learning experience. This may be done in a grade level team, by department at a high school, or by vertical or mixed teams as a professional experience.

Using a protocol to establish behavioral norms guides the discussion and makes the best use of time. Providing behavior prompts and sentence starters can enhance open sharing and more positive engagement (see Figure 7.4). This is especially important while people are gaining confidence in sharing.

Figure 7.4 • Protocol for Collaborative Assessment (Moderation)

Positive Behavior Prompts	Sentence Starter Prompts
• Pose questions to reveal and extend your thinking and to check in on the thinking of others • Pause to allow time for other contributors to reflect before responding. • Share your ideas, inferences, and relevant facts, knowing you can adjust your thinking along the way • Provide specific references to the learning to support your thinking • Distinguish data from interpretation • Presume positive intentions of group members and of the teacher sharing the work	"I see evidence of . . ." "I noticed . . . and it appeared that . . ." "What I perceive from this is . . ." "I'm looking for more evidence of . . ." "Maybe it can be considered another way . . ." "An assumption I am exploring is . . ." "Taking that one step further . . ." "I came to this thought by looking at . . ." "This example made me wonder . . ." "What got me thinking when I looked at . . ." (Gardner, NPDL presentation, 2017)

Source: Adapted from Gardner, M. (2016). Retrieved from www.npdl.global/Deep Learning Hub.

Participants use the behavioral prompts to guide them through the four steps of examining the work.

Step 1: All participants review the learning design and student work independently and use the tools and rubrics to assess both student progress and the quality of the learning design, assessing how well it fostered acquisition of the 6Cs.

Step 2: Participants discuss the learning design and multiple sources of evidence provided in the student work samples and the rubrics. As a group they reach consensus on where they would collectively rate the learning design on the four elements (learning partnerships, learning environments, leveraging digital, and pedagogical practices) and how they would rate the student progress.

Step 3: As teachers moderate the student work to assess progress, they begin to use that data to inform the next steps in student learning.

Step 4: As teachers look more deeply at student progress, they often note that students could have made more progress if the learning experience had been designed differently.

The increased precision in pedagogy that emerges from the deep professional dialogue is building teacher confidence and leading to more innovative practices that meet the relevant needs of all students. The same elements that contribute to deep learning for students have been as crucial for adults.

Learning Redesign

When teachers collaboratively examine learning designs and student progress, they build a deeper understanding of how students learn and how design decisions can influence that learning. The insights have strongly influenced changes in practice and led us to create a protocol for the *learning redesign process* as an extension of the final phase of the collaborative inquiry cycle—*Measure, Reflect, Change.* Learning redesign has become a powerful capacity building approach because as teachers become more transparent in their practice day by day, they see new ways to improve learning designs that will impact their students' progress. The power of this is illustrated in an experience shared by our Australian cluster.

Early in the NPDL journey, Wooranna Park Primary School, State of Victoria, Australia, created their first deep learning unit, titled *The Enigma Mission.* They used the six competencies as a foundation and established learning goals and success criteria that challenged the 10- to 11-year-old students to pursue a passion project using the inquiry model. They captured the student experience on video and noted that students explored a range of areas from paleontology to DNA. The high degree of student engagement, student voice and choice, articulateness of goals, and depth of inquiry are evident in Video 7.1, Wooranna Enigma Mission, at **www.npdl.global**. The final step of the process was to assess collaboratively the student work and progress.

Initially, teachers were very impressed with the passion, ownership, independence, and resourcefulness of the students. As they began to examine the work of the students, they found that while most had excelled when given the choice to select their enigma mission, not all students had achieved to the same degree. As they analyzed the results more deeply, they determined that students who were less successful had not identified as rich an inquiry problem. As they dug deeper, they realized that some students did not possess as wide a world experience as others and that this had hindered them in creating an enigma mission with more scope. Their redesign of the enigma mission deep learning experience is portrayed in Figure 7.5.

Wooranna Park Primary School's Redesign of the Enigma Mission

Teachers determined that they needed to provide a deep learning experience that gave all students a rich foundation for selecting their inquiry.

1. They started with a literacy base linked to the curriculum. Students had a choice of thought provoking novels such as *The Hunger Games* and *I Am Malala*. All the novels related to an overarching theme of interdependence, which is part of the collaboration competency. A wide range of pedagogical practices was used to deepen student thinking such as live forums, symposiums, and Socratic circles.

2. Next, teachers deepened the learning by exploring five themes across all the texts: racism, poverty, government structures affecting change, slavery, and people making a difference. Once again they were deliberate in using a range of pedagogical practices: provocations, immersion videos, excursions, and discussions.

3. Students were supported to make connections and explore different perspectives.

4. At this stage, students then developed their own enigma mission and inquiry question and the method they would use to action their mission. This step came after an extensive range of learning experiences that extended student thinking and options. Again teachers used a range of pedagogical practices including peer review, student-led portfolios, schoolwide feedback, and presentations to an external panel.

5. The final step was moving to action. Students used the research from their enigma mission to develop a way to action their findings in the real world. These actions ranged from working in local soup kitchens and running English lessons for Afghani immigrants to developing films that raise awareness of refugee issues.

Figure 7.5 • Wooranna Park Primary School Redesign: Measure, Reflect, Change

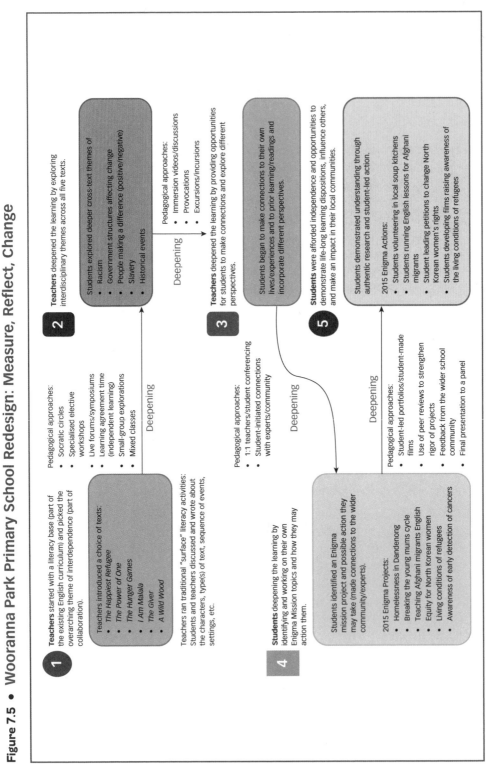

Source: Wooranna Park Primary School, State of Victoria (Department of Education and Training). Thanks to Jennie Vine, Assistant Principal; Anessa Quirit, Grade 5/6 teacher; Grade 5/6 staff 2015; Ray Trotter, Principal; teaching staff, students, parents, and community partners of Grades 5 and 6 during 2015.

This process of learning redesign has been a powerful catalyst for changing practice when all three elements of the final phase of collaborative inquiry are utilized. The Enigma Mission is a vivid example of the powerful precision in pedagogical practices that emerges when teachers have time to collaboratively *measure* student progress using multiple measures of growth, *reflect* on the impact their pedagogy has had on student progress, and then *change* the learning design for a future deep learning experience or use the findings to craft the next learning design in that sequence.

> The deep collaborative work combined with greater transparency of practice is transforming learning design and assessment of student progress.

Final Thoughts

For NPDL, the process of collaborative inquiry has been a powerful catalyst for shifting practice as part of a comprehensive capacity building approach. The deep collaborative work combined with greater transparency of practice is transforming learning design and assessment of student progress. The process of working together to improve the understanding of what learning is and could be, generating evidence of what's working and what is not, and making decisions about next steps leads to improvement and innovation. As they tackle the emerging issues and challenges, educators begin to understand how to achieve both equity and excellence.

In Chapter 8, we turn to the bigger picture by examining the learning conditions and practices in schools, districts, and systems that foster the development of the 6Cs that are needed to propel deep learning. This fourth component of the deep learning framework is essential if we are to move from pockets of innovation to whole system change.

"Culture is like the wind. . . . When it is blowing in your direction, it makes for smooth sailing. When it is blowing against you, everything is more difficult."

—BRYAN WALKER AND SARAH SOULE (2017)

Chapter 8

CONDITIONS THAT MOBILIZE WHOLE SYSTEM CHANGE

What Is Whole System Change?

We define *whole system change* in education as a transformation in the culture of learning. We see the dynamics of whole system change as the interaction of deliberate policies and strategies on the one hand and the occurrence of unpredictable or at least uncontrollable forces (technology being the most prominent) on the other hand. In deep learning we have said that the conditions for whole system change are ripe: The status quo no longer works (the push factor), and the environment is full of attractions and dangers (the pull factor). Something has to give; something fundamental is bound to happen. It is a matter of time and how particular configurations evolve. With our New Pedagogies for Deep Learning (NPDL) partners, we are trying to shape these outcomes for the better.

The mindset we are fostering together is whole system change and deep learning for everyone. It's not about pilots or bolt on programs, but rather it's a rethinking of the learning process. Districts, clusters (networks), or countries all determine how they will begin and how they will expand this rethinking but do so with the perspective that ultimately this is for 100% of the schools. Coherence increases because people see that changing the learning process is integrally tied to all decisions in the organization. Moreover, ongoing "coherence making" is built into processes of continuous collaborative inquiry. Participants begin to link their focused direction to the strategies for cultivating collaborative cultures of learning but are explicit that this is for the purpose of deepening learning. Finally, they are intentional in building the internal capacity to get impact and monitoring progress. Thus the change is systemic not piecemeal.

At the same time, the model is dynamic because it generates innovation and is plugged into an ever-changing external environment. The global partnership has been a catalyst for action and provides rich resources while the members build and share knowledge of both the pedagogical practices that foster deep learning and the organizational conditions that are needed to facilitate transformation. While the global partnership provides a suite of tools and processes that are a catalyst for change, the approach must be driven from within the school, district, cluster, or country. NPDL is not an implementation approach where locals are trained in a program or tool, but rather a facilitation of local capacity that unleashes talent, knowhow, and commitment. This approach builds internal capacity while enabling sustainability. It is a radical change in the culture of schooling.

We think we are making progress for two reasons. One, as we have said, there is a crying need to do something because the current situation does not work for the majority of people. The second is that we have a strong mechanism—a partnership with powerful frameworks, strategies, and tools—to invite, propel, and support progress. In addition to the elements in our framework, we have a modus operandi, or change philosophy, that invites joint determination of the action and its outcomes. The model is intended to "liberate" the actions of those at the next level down (e.g., districts compared to states; principals to districts; teachers to students) and view policies upward as things to be exploited for local purpose. Finally, the model is laced with lateral and vertical two-way learning. In short hand we say liberate downward, exploit upward, and learn every which way. And do so with purpose: the 6Cs, learning design, reduce inequality, and increase excellence. This model has the characteristics of a social or cultural movement in which people are attracted to new ideas that connect with or activate basic unmet needs or values and promise dramatic new outcomes.

Transforming practice requires a multidimensional approach that fosters new understandings, knowledge, and skills at all levels. This growth orientation means that capacity is built through job-embedded learning that occurs over time rather than at events. We define *capacity building* as the process that develops the ability of individuals and groups to make the changes needed to improve. Successful organizations articulate clearly the knowledge, skills, and attributes needed to make the change and provide opportunities for collaborative learning to occur. This often includes developing skill and knowledge in change leadership, building relationships, precision in pedagogy, and using data to assess progress. The global partnership has modeled this sustained job-embedded learning with and from peers. Leadership from the partner countries is used to bring on new members.

The partnership personifies the notion of *go outside to get better inside* by creating opportunities for knowledge building that promote within-school, across-school, and cross-organization connections. A range of collective capacity building sessions, global events, deep learning challenges, and moderation of learning experiences and student results, both locally and globally, are designed to build common language and deepen knowledge as educators and students collaborate over time and space.

All in all, given the disruption of the change we are talking about, it has had a rapid start. We would call it a *go slow to go fast* proposition—lots of questions at the beginning, a sense that there is great new value accompanied by

---

Liberate downward, exploit upward, and learn every which way—and do so with purpose: the 6Cs, learning design, reduce inequality, and increase excellence.

Go outside to get better inside.

a burst of energy. Like most social movements, and because of the strategy we employ, there is a strong contagion factor—locally and globally.

Learning Conditions That Foster Deep Learning

Our overall model includes the conditions and practices that need to be in place in schools, districts, and systems if deep learning is to take root. These conditions (see Figure 8.1) form a circle of support for the uptake of deep learning competencies and the use of the four elements for designing deep learning.

Figure 8.1 • Deep Learning Conditions

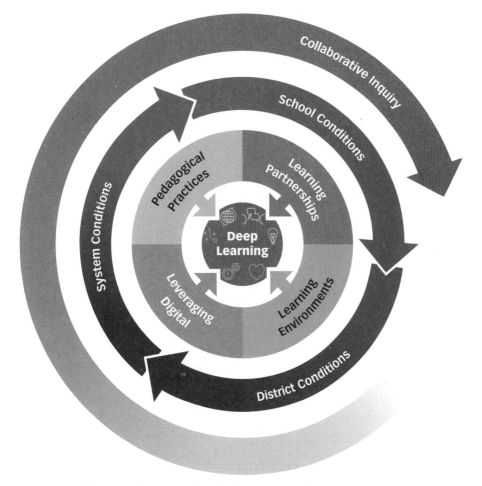

Source: Copyright © 2014 by New Pedagogies for Deep Learning™ (NPDL)

Leading transformation change is complex, and sustainability is fragile. While we don't see whole systems on the move yet, we are seeing glimpses of promising progress. Five conditions and their subdimensions that impact the take up of deep learning are identified in the following box.

> **Five Learning Conditions That Impact the Diffusion of Deep Learning**
>
> Vision and Goals
>
> - Goals and clarity of strategy
>
> Leadership
>
> - Leadership capacity
> - Role of lead learners
> - Change leadership
>
> Collaborative Cultures
>
> - Culture of learning
> - Collaborative work
> - Capacity building
>
> Deepening the Learning
>
> - Global competencies
> - Precision in the new pedagogies
> - Processes to shift practice
>
> New Measures and Evaluation
>
> - New tools and methods of measurement
> - Mechanisms to measure impact

We have created a Deep Learning Conditions Rubric to describe the practices related to each of the five dimensions. The rubric provides descriptors for four levels of progress. Teams use the rubric to identify evidence that they are providing the conditions for deep learning. Figure 8.2 provides a sample rubric that is used by schools and districts to assess current strengths and needs, identify areas that need to be addressed if deep learning is to flourish, and measure progress on each condition over time. The system policy issues are not incorporated into this rubric but are addressed later in this chapter.

Analyzing the evidence generated when using the rubric provides multiple perspectives from a team. For example, the district may feel that it is providing effective capacity building, while teachers may perceive that they need more help from coaches to embed the new ideas in their daily practice. The deep dialogue that occurs helps clarify both the strengths that are supporting innovation and the gaps. Once teams have highlighted a profile of their current status, they can look to higher levels on the rubric to inform their next steps. Schools most often use the rubric at the beginning and end of each year to assess progress and make plans for the coming cycle. The

Figure 8.2 • Deep Learning Conditions Rubric

Dimensions	Limited	Emerging	Accelerating	Advanced
Vision and Goals	There are no deep learning strategies, goals or implementation supports in place to achieve deep learning. Decisions and resources reflect the status quo.	Deep learning strategies and goals are formally written and articulated. Some decisions regarding resources, processes, and funding reflect a shift toward deep learning.	There is a written and understood strategy articulating deep learning goals and how they will be implemented. Most decisions are driven by and aligned with deep learning.	A concise, well-articulated strategy with focused deep learning goals and implementation support is owned by all members of the school community and used to drive decision making.
Leadership	Leaders rely on formal roles and structures and view deep learning as an add-on rather than integrator and accelerator of processes. There is no strategy to intentionally develop leaders at all levels, and engagement in deep learning is restricted to a few early innovators.	Lead learners are emerging across the school who clearly see their role in developing leaders, structures, processes, and formal and informal opportunities, all committed to fostering deep learning. Student, teacher, family, and community engagement in deep learning is emerging.	Lead learners have created structures and processes that propel shifts in practice and intentionally develop leaders at all levels. There is engagement in deep learning across the school and among some students, families, and communities who actively take part in the creation of deep learning experiences.	Lead learner capacity exists at *all* levels, with a clear strategy to develop, diffuse, and distribute leadership capacity across the school. Students, families, teachers, leaders, and members of the community are informed, engaged, and influential in deep learning for all students.
Collaborative Cultures	Collaboration between and among leaders, teachers, and learners occurs through formal structures without challenging "the way we do things around here." Inquiry is practiced inconsistently, and low levels of trust are reflected in an unwillingness to share practices and ideas. Capacity building support often focuses on individual needs and is not explicitly linked to deep learning.	There is an emerging collaborative culture developed around deep learning and collective capacity building. Leaders and teachers are using collaborative inquiry to reflect on existing practices, and there are some structures and processes for building vertical and horizontal relationships and learning across the school and district. Resourcing to support collaboration is emerging but may not always be focused, connected, or consistently used to foster deep learning.	A culture of learning and collaborative inquiry exists in which most teachers and leaders reflect on, review, and adjust their teaching and leadership practices. Capacity building is designed based on teacher and student needs and is clearly focused on the knowledge and skills needed to mobilize and sustain deep learning. Through vertical and horizontal relationships, collaboration and trust are growing and practices are becoming more transparent. School-level inquiry and learning involve leaders and teachers from all levels, and teachers may also be collaborating across schools.	A powerful culture of collaborative deep learning pervades the school and district. Learning collaboratively is the norm and includes structures and processes to build collective capacity. The culture uses the group to change the group by fostering strong vertical and horizontal relationships that support innovation and risk taking. Capacity building focuses comprehensively and consistently on precision in pedagogy and incorporates cycles of learning and application within and across the school and with other schools.

(Continued)

Figure 8.2 • (Continued)

Dimensions	Limited	Emerging	Accelerating	Advanced
Deepening the Learning	The relationship between school curriculum and deep learning competencies is unspecified. A framework for deep learning is beginning to develop but is not understood by all or used consistently to guide learning. Individual teachers and leaders are innovating independently. Few coaches and personnel are dedicated to supporting deep learning. Collaborative practices such as collaborative inquiry and moderation are not well understood and are used infrequently.	The relationship between Deep learning and local curriculum is beginning to be articulated. Some goals to improve precision in pedagogy have been identified but the strategy for improvement may be unclear or implemented inconsistently. Deep collaborative practices such as collaborative inquiry and protocols for examining student work may be used by some teachers or some schools but there is not consistency of practice or support.	Learning and pedagogical goals are articulated and the link between deep learning competencies and core curriculum standards is visible. A comprehensive framework for deep learning is used widely to design and assess deep learning experiences. Resources and expertise for creating collaborative learning structures are becoming more consistent across the school/ district, as are deep collaborative practices such as collaborative inquiry and protocols for examining student work.	Learning goals for deep learning competencies, goals to improve precision in pedagogy, and requirements of core curriculum standards are clearly articulated and integrated consistently with visible impact. A comprehensive framework for deep learning is understood by all and used consistently across the school and district to design and assess effective deep learning experiences. Collaborative inquiry is used to monitor progress in impacting learning at all levels, and protocols for examining student work are used consistently across the school and district.
New Measures and Evaluation	Evaluation of student success and achievement continues to rely on a narrow range of indicators (e.g., tests and a small number of work products) to measure and track success. Teachers and school leaders may be using the New Measures to develop a shared language and understanding of deep learning, but deep learning conditions, design, and outcomes are not yet measured or assessed.	Mixed-method assessment practice is beginning to develop, as a wider and more diverse range of evidence sources is used to measure and track progress and success. Capacity building supports for using the New Measures and designing meaningful assessments are beginning to develop. Some teachers and leaders are beginning to use the New Measures to design deep learning experiences, measure student outcomes, and measure conditions for deep learning.	Teachers and leaders demonstrate the capacity to assess, develop, and measure • Student growth on the Deep Learning Progressions • Conditions that enable deep learning to occur • The effectiveness of deep learning design in facilitating deep learning outcomes Local and national priorities and curriculum are linked to and accelerated by deep learning experiences, which are moderated through a structured process. Teachers are beginning to design new assessments for deep learning that more clearly demonstrate deep learning as it occurs.	The development and measurement of deep learning is pervasive throughout the school and district, and used to focus capacity building efforts. Measures are compared across years and time periods and demonstrate consistent growth. Deep learning experiences demonstrate clear alignment between curriculum and deep learning goals and are formally moderated both within and between schools to establish reliability. Feedback is shared and leveraged to deepen learning design. Assessment practice reflects a deep knowledge of students' interests and needs and uses a wide range of evidence to determine progress and learning.

Source: Quinn, J., & McEachen, J. Copyright © 2017 by New Pedagogies for Deep Learning™ (NPDL)

iterative process of *do, reflect, adjust* is changing the way they view change and making the use of evidence to track progress more explicit.

The New Change Dynamic

A new change dynamic is emerging in schools and systems that are moving toward deep learning. A shift away from an implementation mindset of "rolling out" to a more organic process of co-learning and co-development is taking root. It is crucial to note that learning occurs laterally (within and across schools, districts, and systems) much more so than in traditional hierarchical schooling. We have observed three phases of change as schools, districts, and countries have taken up deep learning (see Figure 8.3).

A shift away from an implementation mindset of "rolling out" to a more organic process of co-learning and co-development is taking root.

Figure 8.3 • Phases of the New Change Dynamic

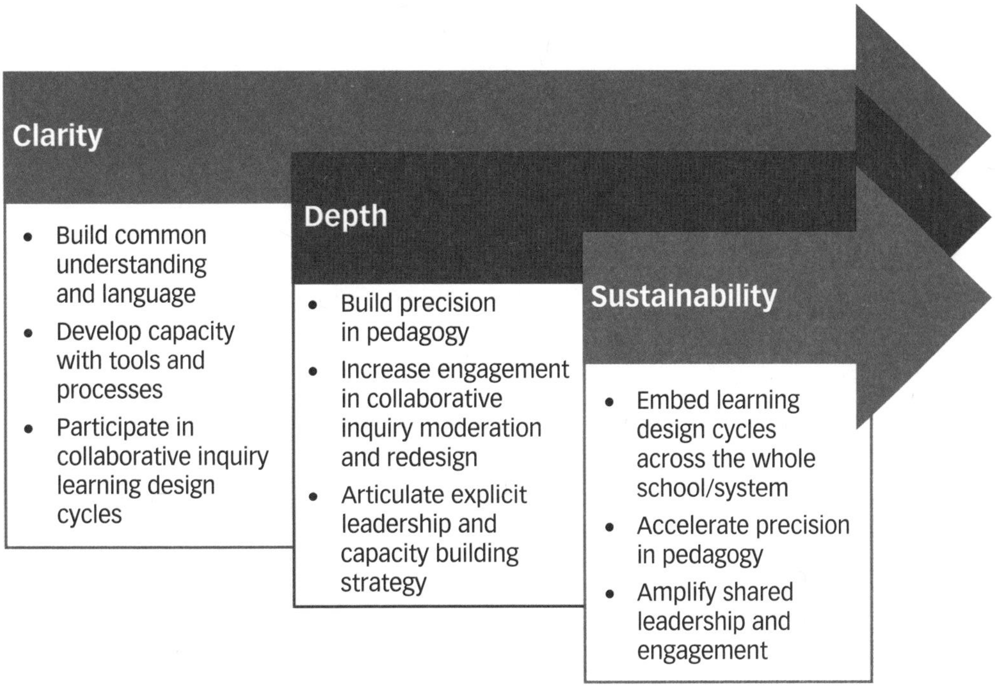
Clarity
• Build common understanding and language
• Develop capacity with tools and processes
• Participate in collaborative inquiry learning design cycles
Depth
• Build precision in pedagogy
• Increase engagement in collaborative inquiry moderation and redesign
• Articulate explicit leadership and capacity building strategy
Sustainability
• Embed learning design cycles across the whole school/system
• Accelerate precision in pedagogy
• Amplify shared leadership and engagement

Phase I: Clarity

The first phase of deep learning work involves establishing clarity of focus, shared understandings, and expertise. Clarity is a process as much as it is a state. Grass roots efforts often emerge from the passion of teachers or leaders who are ready to embrace different ways of working. Everyone has a different starting point. Rapid innovation is fostered and feeds into establishing a clear, shared vision of what deep learning might look like and sound like in the classroom. As teachers and leaders begin to use the new approaches and share results, they need a mechanism to *learn from the work*. The focused discussions and examination of current and future practice reinforce the new vision for learning. The collaborative inquiry process begins to guide the examination of pedagogical practices and assessment of student progress. At this stage it is critical to build trust and transparency. As teachers become more transparent in sharing their practice, they need to feel safe to share their successes and challenges without fear of judgment. As the sharing evolves, schools often feel the need to reorganize structures to create time and space for teacher collaborative inquiry. They engage in rich dialogue examining pedagogical practices that deepen learning and look carefully at how well students are learning and how to improve. At the same time, they begin to approach parents as partners, finding ways to listen to and respond to their concerns while also engaging them in the new learning practices. One of the most powerful impacts on this early stage is seeing the visible changes in their students. They observe significant increases in engagement and results as they use the deep learning approaches. Leaders who wish to encourage deep learning

- give teachers risk-free opportunities to see their students change before their eyes;
- make time for teachers who have experienced the power of deep learning in their classrooms to share their stories;
- encourage visits to other classrooms and schools where this new approach is taking root; and
- facilitate virtual connections with other schools and practitioners who are a few months further on the journey.

Phase II: Depth

The second phase usually evolves when teachers and leaders have developed a working, collective vision of the competencies and have developed initial skills in using the four elements to design deep learning experiences. Mechanisms are needed to intentionally *learn from the work*, gain precision in collaborative examination of practice, and increase precision in pedagogy. In this phase, teachers and leaders have participated in at least one collaborative inquiry cycle and as a result are motivated to develop even greater precision in selecting pedagogical practices and in scaffolding experiences so their students will move to higher levels of progress in acquiring the competencies. Collectively, they begin to engage in more frequent collaborative inquiry cycles to design new learning experiences and also to moderate the progress of their students. Teacher leadership is amplified as because they seek opportunities to learn within and outside the school. Capacity building for teachers and leaders is job embedded with external inputs as needed. This increased precision and intentionality is observed in both student and adult learning experiences.

Phase III: Sustainability

Once a level of expertise is attained, the focus shifts to deepening the work and spreading it more widely. Schools, districts, and systems consider how to integrate their strategies so that coherence is built. In our global work, we have observed that once teachers develop confidence and expertise in designing and assessing deep learning and working effectively in collaborative inquiry cycles, they shift their focus to helping others change. This happens in two ways. First, the focus moves to going deeper, which involves greater precision in learning designs and moderation cycles. Second, districts and clusters move to embed the collaborative practices across more schools and ultimately the entire system. Strong teacher and school leadership evolves to guide the next steps. They not only continue to explore the best ways to develop and measure the six competencies but also set internal targets for the school or system. In effect, all this amounts to continuous professional learning the way it should be—built into the culture.

> In effect, all this amounts to continuous professional learning the way it should be—built into the culture.

The NPDL cluster in Victoria, Australia, developed a solid foundation in deep learning in the first 3 years of engagement but has identified three issues they are working on that are indicative of the deeper dive that begins to occur in Phase III.

- **Improving assessment practices**—We plan to strengthen teacher's confidence and capability to employ agile, contemporary assessment practices. We need to create opportunities to expand the repertoire of teacher and learner assessment strategies as part of the ongoing process of capturing, analyzing, and interpreting data and evidence about student progress.

- **System curriculum frameworks**—Helping teachers think outside the box of curriculum and overcome the "We can't do this because we are given what we have to teach!" stance is a next challenge. System frameworks are often perceived as nonnegotiable system structures that constrain innovation. Many teachers have a perception that things can only be done one way when they actually have freedom to plan their curriculum more flexibly than they think. The Curriculum Framework in Victoria identifies "what to teach" and not how to teach. Our Curriculum Authority describes the curriculum as "the what" the students should actually learn the rest is up to teachers. The expectation is that schools and teachers will turn it into "the how." The curriculum is not the pedagogy, it is what we want all young people to have the opportunity to understand and apply. How teachers implement that in their classroom and the decisions they make as a whole school around the issues of pedagogy is completely up to the school. It should be based on local context, local needs and local expertise but that doesn't take away from "what." Supporting teachers to increase their confidence and capability to identify, implement, and experiment with new and/or proven pedagogical practices needs to continue if we are to consolidate, sustain, and spread deep learning in their schools and beyond.

(Continued)

(Continued)

- **Not underestimating students**—Preconceived ideas about what students should be able to do sometimes limits the breadth of opportunities teachers make available. We are constantly in awe of some of the learnings and subsequent outputs from students when teachers scaffold learning, but provide open-ended challenges. (personal communication, May 2017)

In Phase III, local leadership owns the strategy, takes initiative to go deeper, and spreads the practices more widely. They regularly go outside to get better inside, connecting across schools, districts, and the globe. They are intentional about developing leaders at all levels, especially teacher leaders and, most important, are looking for impact and learning constantly from the work.

Social movements are about ideas and often begin with early innovators who are passionate about change.

Deep Learning in Action

Social movements are about ideas and often begin with early innovators who are passionate about change. We look next to examples of how the conditions and practices are unfolding in schools, districts, and systems.

Schools on the Move

The next example comes from one of six high schools in **Queensland, Australia**, who wanted to join the deep learning work and formed a cluster of schools to learn and share from each other.

Go Outside to Get Better Inside

Pine River Secondary School; Queensland, Australia

Pine River began with a small group of committed teaches but rapidly linked deep learning to the overall strategic plan for the school and used deep learning to amplify the change. They engaged their staff by aligning their planning documents with the tools and common language of NPDL, developing a shared understanding of deep learning at the outset of their work with NPDL, adopting the Collaborative Inquiry Cycle, and developing a "sharp and narrow" implementation focus. The notion of *go outside to get better inside* was crucial because they met regularly with the other six high schools to share practice and insights. This note from the principal about 8 months into the process describes the impact on the school.

> NPDL has had such an impact on my staff that our 2017 explicit improvement agenda is "The deep learning process." We have shaped our planning documents to capture the three conditions

CHAPTER 8

needed for deep learning: deep learning goals; explicit pedagogies accelerated through digital; and capacity building of staff. You can see how the strategic vision of the school aligns with our NPDL journey. I have also aligned our planning to show cohesion with ASOT and the National Standards for teachers. (See Figure 8.4.)

We started with curriculum opportunities for our students through STEM and HASS project based units in Grades 7 and 8 and deeper opportunities in our signature "IGNITE" program. This is an application-based program. However the most exciting piece of work is the designing of our "Learning for Life" program across Grades 7 and 12. This program will develop the 6Cs competencies in a range of selected personal development programs. The staff voted to re-structure our timetable to allow a daily time where we will explicitly teach students the skills around the 6Cs. Even as we wind down for Xmas planning teams are discussing the program. I walked into our creative thinking group huddled around the rubrics debating the conditions outlined in the document. A teacher who has been a late adopter to NPDL even suggested not taking the holiday but starting to dig deeper. I can honestly say this year, working with our NPDL cluster, has been some of the best work I have been part of in my 32 years of education. (John Shnur, principal, Pine River Secondary School, Queensland, personal communication, December 2016)

Fast forward 6 months later and a second note arrived from Principal Shnur describing Pine River's first mandatory major school review conducted by the Queensland State Schools. It was the first review of a school that had *Deep Learning* as its explicit improvement agenda. The principal related:

The reviewers are trained to come into schools and focus on Literacy and Numeracy. They weren't quite sure how to deal with us and took a day of questioning before they realized we were focusing on an approach that didn't fit their brief. We have done a lot of work around mapping the 6Cs to the 21st Century Skills and General Capabilities that underpin our National Curriculum. This helped in cementing the validity of our work.

By Day 4, they were all won over and our review results were outstanding. Interestingly, it was our community partnerships that did the trick. Particularly when the Professor at the University, which works with one of our Deep Learning projects, said the greatest complement he could give was that they have learnt more from our students and teachers then they have taught them. The reviewers recognized that our Learning for Life program is in its infancy but congratulated us on having the courage to explicitly teach the competencies across the school.

Figure 8.4 • Pine River Annual Improvement Plan 2017

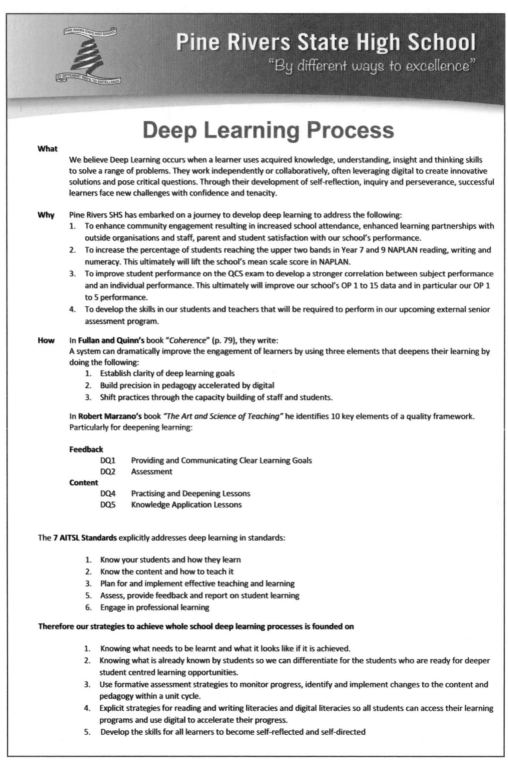

Pine Rivers State High School
"By different ways to excellence"

Deep Learning Process

What

We believe Deep Learning occurs when a learner uses acquired knowledge, understanding, insight and thinking skills to solve a range of problems. They work independently or collaboratively, often leveraging digital to create innovative solutions and pose critical questions. Through their development of self-reflection, inquiry and perseverance, successful learners face new challenges with confidence and tenacity.

Why   Pine Rivers SHS has embarked on a journey to develop deep learning to address the following:

1. To enhance community engagement resulting in increased school attendance, enhanced learning partnerships with outside organisations and staff, parent and student satisfaction with our school's performance.
2. To increase the percentage of students reaching the upper two bands in Year 7 and 9 NAPLAN reading, writing and numeracy. This ultimately will lift the school's mean scale score in NAPLAN.
3. To improve student performance on the QCS exam to develop a stronger correlation between subject performance and an individual performance. This ultimately will improve our school's OP 1 to 15 data and in particular our OP 1 to 5 performance.
4. To develop the skills in our students and teachers that will be required to perform in our upcoming external senior assessment program.

How   In **Fullan and Quinn's** book *"Coherence"* (p. 79), they write:

A system can dramatically improve the engagement of learners by using three elements that deepens their learning by doing the following:

1. Establish clarity of deep learning goals
2. Build precision in pedagogy accelerated by digital
3. Shift practices through the capacity building of staff and students.

In **Robert Marzano's** book *"The Art and Science of Teaching"* he identifies 10 key elements of a quality framework. Particularly for deepening learning:

Feedback
      DQ1   Providing and Communicating Clear Learning Goals
      DQ2   Assessment
Content
      DQ4   Practising and Deepening Lessons
      DQ5   Knowledge Application Lessons

The **7 AITSL Standards** explicitly addresses deep learning in standards:

1. Know your students and how they learn
2. Know the content and how to teach it
3. Plan for and implement effective teaching and learning
5. Assess, provide feedback and report on student learning
6. Engage in professional learning

Therefore our strategies to achieve whole school deep learning processes is founded on

1. Knowing what needs to be learnt and what it looks like if it is achieved.
2. Knowing what is already known by students so we can differentiate for the students who are ready for deeper student centred learning opportunities.
3. Use formative assessment strategies to monitor progress, identify and implement changes to the content and pedagogy within a unit cycle.
4. Explicit strategies for reading and writing literacies and digital literacies so all students can access their learning programs and use digital to accelerate their progress.
5. Develop the skills for all learners to become self-reflected and self-directed

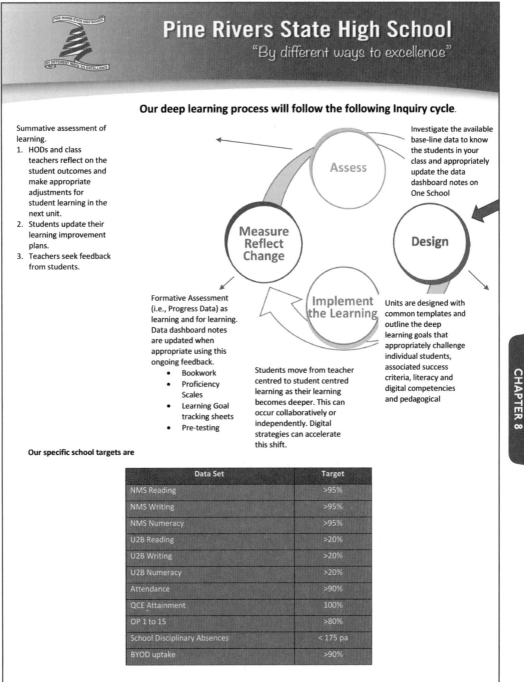

Pine Rivers State High School
"By different ways to excellence"

Our deep learning process will follow the following Inquiry cycle.

Summative assessment of learning.
1. HODs and class teachers reflect on the student outcomes and make appropriate adjustments for student learning in the next unit.
2. Students update their learning improvement plans.
3. Teachers seek feedback from students.

Assess

Investigate the available base-line data to know the students in your class and appropriately update the data dashboard notes on One School

Measure Reflect Change

Design

Implement the Learning

Formative Assessment (i.e., Progress Data) as learning and for learning. Data dashboard notes are updated when appropriate using this ongoing feedback.
- Bookwork
- Proficiency Scales
- Learning Goal tracking sheets
- Pre-testing

Students move from teacher centred to student centred learning as their learning becomes deeper. This can occur collaboratively or independently. Digital strategies can accelerate this shift.

Units are designed with common templates and outline the deep learning goals that appropriately challenge individual students, associated success criteria, literacy and digital competencies and pedagogical

Our specific school targets are

Data Set	Target
NMS Reading	>95%
NMS Writing	>95%
NMS Numeracy	>95%
U2B Reading	>20%
U2B Writing	>20%
U2B Numeracy	>20%
Attendance	>90%
QCE Attainment	100%
OP 1 to 15	>80%
School Disciplinary Absences	< 175 pa
BYOD uptake	>90%

Source: Courtesy of John Shnur, principal, Pine River Secondary School, Queensland

This is one of scores of schools on the move. What is remarkable is that this significant shift across a whole high school has occurred in 18 months. Districts, states, and education systems see the great impact the new approaches are having on students but are struggling to match their traditional measures of impact with the new reality. We are working with our country partners to identify better ways to demonstrate not just the acquisition of the competencies but the ways in which these students are better prepared for life. While contexts, capacity, and resources vary, we are seeing that a focused vision of deep learning combined with a comprehensive set of tools and practices is accelerating change. We look next at how to move from single innovative schools to whole systems of schools on the move.

Districts on the Move

Districts play a vital role in enabling the conditions that foster a shift to deep learning mindsets and practices while removing barriers to promote the spread of practices across whole systems. Districts can propel change when they

- focus the system on deep learning with a whole system mindset,

- cultivate a culture of innovation and collaboration where students and adults feel safe and supported to take risks and learn from failures and successes,

- intentionally build precision in pedagogy by providing opportunities for capacity building, and

- establish criteria for measuring success.

There is no recipe for moving to deep learning. We consider the next two district stories, Kern Unified in **California** and Ottawa Catholic District School Board in **Canada**. Each represents a dramatically different context and journey, but both illustrate the importance of the district role in establishing conditions for change.

Shifting the Community to a Global Mindset

Southern Kern Unified District; Kern, California

Visit Southern Kern Unified (SKUD), a small district serving 3,500 students, and you can't help but notice the pride and enthusiasm that parents, students, teachers, and leaders have for the district. SKUD has been engaged with NPDL for less than a year, so we consider this a startup example. It wasn't always like that. Southern Kern is a remote, small community at the southern desert-end of the California Central Valley serving a student population that is predominantly Hispanic and White with 90% of students eligible for free and reduced lunch. The physical isolation strikes you immediately. It is surrounded by space, horizontally and vertically, with Edwards Air Force Base in close proximity and closely regulated.

Superintendent Weinstein describes the community attitude in a curiously powerful way. "When I arrived and started to talk about reimagining education and the possibilities for our kids, the community response was—No . . . we couldn't do that. We are just a Mom and Pop store here . . . not like the big cities . . . that's way beyond us." Weinstein persisted, seeking every opportunity for connecting schools and students to community, ensuring that new facilities were built, existing ones updated, and that students had every opportunity to engage in new and exciting ways of learning, connected to each other, their aspirations, and others outside the schools' physical boundaries.

Then in August 2016, Southern Kern joined NPDL, a global partnership of seven countries devoted to fostering deep learning for all. Soon every student, teacher, and leader was engaged in the work of deep learning. During the year, every student participated in a deep learning experience. The common theme was Collaboration, and it drove not only the learning, but also the district itself. The leadership team intentionally grew networks, formed partnerships, and sought every opportunity to engage community. Superintendent Weinstein points to NPDL as a key to this new culture and to proving that the entire Southern Kern community could be a part of something more than a mom and pop storefront, and in fact collaborate, communicate, and learn as part of the global knowledge economy. Visit the community and you will hear that students are connecting and learning in ways they never have before. Parent and community engagement are at all-time highs. There is a sense above all of expanded horizons and purpose. Their enthusiasm and commitment are palpable. Their leadership is finely attuned. Their learning is inspiring.

The speed of take up in Southern Kern has been remarkable and illustrates the power of contagion when the *mindset is whole system change* and a district *goes outside to get better inside*. The deep learning agenda has served as a catalyst for integrating the work of the district and has unleashed engagement of students, teachers, and community alike, who are now seeing themselves as part of a global movement. We don't yet consider Kern to be an example of deep change because it is too early, but the initial success reinforces our finding that change can be propelled rapidly when the conditions are right.

The second district vignette describes an intentional social movement to go districtwide over a 3-year period. Ottawa Catholic is an urban school district serving more than 40,000 students in 84 schools. Not every school and classroom is fully immersed in deep learning; yet visiting the district and its schools provides a glimpse into what is possible.

System Change Unleashed

Ottawa Catholic District School Board; Ottawa, Canada

Walk into schools and you see students working with their own personal devices and using space purposefully for collaborating or moving. They may be using green walls scattered throughout the building to create videos so that they can add backgrounds and audio later. Walls are covered with colorful student-made products and art. There is a buzz of engagement, and students taking responsibility for their learning is the norm.

But it's not just the students who are learning in new ways. Teaching and learning are highly visible with teachers meeting in teams by grade or cross panel to plan learning activities or examine the depth of student learning and work. Teacher learning isn't restricted to planning, because you will see schools where teachers are learning alongside or directly from students as they explore ideas, new digital devices, or resources that are not familiar to the teachers.

Principal and district leaders are also visible learners because they attend student-led workshops or tutoring sessions to learn how to leverage digital to enhance their own learning or pedagogical practice. Participation in learning walks, where teams of teachers, leaders, and sometimes students visit classrooms with an observational purpose, sharpens skills of both observing classroom practice and providing feedback to deepen student learning. At the same time, monthly meetings of all principals and district leaders are opportunities to focus on sharing and developing solutions to problems of practice

Making this kind of learning the norm for all schools and classrooms doesn't happen by chance. Ottawa Catholic embraced the deep learning agenda and used the components of the coherence framework to craft a whole system strategy for change. The district leaders describe the conditions that have contributed to their journey.

Leadership and governance—setting the stage. Innovation and well-being were already at the heart of change in this district. Beginning in 2010, a collaboratively created blueprint for change focused on a cultural shift across the board while the creation of a digital ecosystem focused more on staff and student collaboration, creativity, critical thinking, and communication. Simultaneously, the district improved infrastructure, including Wi-Fi in all schools, conversion of school libraries to learning commons, laptops for all educators, and integrated software and hardware supports. Governance issues were integrated with the creation of a social media policy as well as the first plan in the province to integrate yearly instruction on digital citizenship into the curriculum. Leaders were intentional in building on these foundations to strategically craft a coherent plan for whole system change over 3 years (2014–2017) and to divert funds to directly support this new direction. It is important to note that the strong implementation was achieved without new money but by focusing direction and realigning resources to support it.

Whole system mindset. The senior leadership team of the district recognized that NPDL was aligned with the board's focus on pedagogy as a driver and leveraging technology to create new learning and teaching opportunities. Strategically, the first set of seven schools was selected to participate in NPDL. Schools were selected based on one per academic superintendent's family of schools to ensure that all superintendents were part of the leadership process along with a school in each trustee's zone. Each superintendent selected a school that had a supportive principal and a staff that had demonstrated a commitment to the change process that had been initiated with the creation of a digital ecosystem. To build capacity, each school was matched with one central staff member and also with one teacher from another school that was already part of a learning network called *learning connections*. Learning connection teachers were taking part in a provincial learning network that supported educators with access to applications, technology, professional learning, and collaboration opportunities. In this way we were able to gain synergies by connecting multiple learning networks. A central staff member was assigned to lead this new NPDL learning network, and she became the board champion to support and promote NPDL.

In 2015, the second year, the board built on the early successes of the NPDL learning network by expanding to 15 schools and by creating a virtual connection of five intermediate schools, for a total of 20 participating schools. Leadership from the middle became important, as the work of staff involved in Year One schools was leveraged to spread the work in new schools. The model of connecting schools with one central staff member and with one teacher from another school was continued. The inquiry cycle model was used and culminated in a successful learning fair where staff celebrated and shared their successes using the NPDL framework.

An important system structure was created in that year, the central coherence committee. Senior leaders had previously encouraged interdepartmental work to try to align initiatives including the NPDL learning network. The view that function trumps structure was evident in the creation of the central coherence committee because a more nimble and strategic committee focused on coherence rather than alignment.

Capacity building as a priority. The capacity building that had taken place in Years One and Two was important to be able to move to the engagement of all 84 schools in year three. No longer would NPDL be viewed as a separate learning network, but rather it would be viewed as the board's learning and

(Continued)

teaching framework for all learning networks. All central staff built their capacity in using the deep learning framework with a specific focus on the terminology of the four learning design elements and the six global competencies of deep learning. Learning networks such as numeracy, literacy, and kindergarten would continue, but each would use a framework of deep learning in their practice. As a Catholic school system it was important for us to bring our Catholic language into the definitions and approaches to teaching global competencies. Given the focus on real-life problem solving and social action, the link to Catholic graduate expectations was a seamless process.

Cultivate action based on collaborative inquiry. Each superintendent would use the school conditions rubric as a discussion point for reflecting on school innovation when they met with the school principals they supported. The existing NPDL champion would remain involved and would use her expertise to bring the deep learning process to all new teachers and to the various coaching and professional learning groups throughout the board. All staff throughout the board would receive a deep learning reference guide so that they would see the language of deep learning and the coherent approach to our focus on literacy and numeracy achievement. The director of education would include deep learning as a focus in all systemwide addresses and in the monthly meeting with school principals and system leaders. Each learning network would use a rubric based on deep learning as a method for monitoring and reflecting on the system impact of their work.

Educators who were involved in Year One or Year Two of NPDL now have an opportunity to participate in a deep learning certificate program where they mentor educators from another school through an inquiry cycle, taking advantage of the toolkit of rubrics for teaching and measuring global competencies. These early adopters will be rewarded with digital badges in recognition of their work. A separate introduction to deep learning course has been created for staff who want to accelerate their implementation of deep learning in their classrooms.

Go outside to get better inside. At the central level, we are achieving coherence because we now have departments working together and implementing their collective work using the same teaching and learning network. School staff has the same lexicon that enables them to work collaboratively and connect learning networks. Leadership is coming from all areas of the organization, and school visits and learning walks are focusing on the four elements and six global competencies.

Ottawa Catholic has not only changed within but also offered leadership to global partners by hosting visits to their classrooms and sharing a range of resources they have created. In their own words, "Students and staff are energized with the Board focus on Deep Learning. We are successfully 'using the group to move the group.'" (personal communication, December 2016)

In both district examples, we see that the whole system mindset is crucial to the rapidity and depth of change. Initially, each had vastly different contexts and resources, yet both were able to create a compelling vision and strategy for change that builds capacity in an iterative way by creating conditions for innovation and learning from the work. Finally, NPDL districts (Ottawa being a prime example) become active with other schools and districts because they receive visitors, help other systems, and participate in regional and global NPDL learning labs.

Systems on the Move

We are working in seven countries with large clusters of schools, so the question arises of whether entire countries can change. There is no jurisdiction that we know of that has created the superstructure to support deep learning across an entire provincial, state, or national system. Frankly, we don't know whether this is the way to go. We have been content to help create and/or work with the whole system without defining the work as a "government project." We have identified the components that must be addressed and what systems need to do to stimulate and support the evolution of deep learning. The most obvious elements at the system level include articulation of deep learning as a valued goal, curriculum policies, infrastructure, investment, capacity support strategies, and assessment systems that align with deep learning outcomes. Governments must ensure that high-quality ubiquitous access to the digital world is available to all. State policies that embrace deep learning experiences and incorporate them into curriculum frameworks are happening in a number of places. The role of systems is to legitimize, support, and enable schools and districts to engage and embrace deep learning. This includes investing in strategies that foster innovation and having rich mechanisms for the center to learn continually from what is being tried. One key structure is to sponsor and legitimize cross-boundary partnerships and learning through networks and clusters of schools and districts. Another strategy is to actively support and facilitate business-school partnerships and partnerships with other community groups and across the global spectrum.

The transformation of public policy must also address the issue of assessment discussed in this chapter and addressed more extensively in Chapter 9, where we note that confining the focus of teaching and learning to what is easily measurable actually narrows the teaching and learning. Education systems must look at what learning content and outcomes are important for success in today's world. This necessitates a transformative shift in measurement tools and practices. It means developing reliable measures of deep learning, as well as effective methods to capture and assess deep learning skills in the everyday work of students. The solution needs to focus on both internal and external accountability. *Internal accountability* refers to the development of collective responsibility for student learning among teachers and school leaders. Individuals and groups define the learning goals relative to state policy, seamlessly link learning and assessment, and are transparent and specific about what is happening and with what impact. *External accountability* reinforces performance related to new measures.

In the Appendix, we provide snapshots of each of the seven countries and in Chapter 6 we featured deep learning examples. Our purpose is to give some context and flesh to the nature of the work.

Final Thoughts

Overall, our conclusion is, and we think participants in the seven countries would agree, that NPDL is a strong low cost–high yield foray into system-level deep learning. But the story should not end there. There is still the question of how stable our NPDL movement has become. Turnover in leadership over any 5-year period or less can be pretty much guaranteed, so we encouraged the building of teams of leaders and related widespread concentration of support. We think this has contributed to the multiyear commitment we are experiencing, but we see in a few cases where the support has not been wide or deep enough. Change is fragile, and efforts must be sustained.

There is also a case to be made that the status quo may be immovable from within. We have done our best by empowering the bottom and not relying on the top. The tough question is, even if educators have the commitment to change, will they be able to do so in the face of their own habits and dispositions and/or pressures from the system related to ongoing norms? Our colleague Richard Elmore from Harvard, a vigilant and perspicacious student of school and system improvement over many decades, sent us the following response to our basic argument: "Fundamentally, institutionalized thinking tends to project the future in ways that are compatible with existing, predictable structures" (Elmore, personal communication, 2017). And related to our third and equally deep reason, Elmore added, "Society is increasingly morphing into something much less rigidly defined and much more lateral and networked."

Lateral and networked learning is essential to our strategy, but we take Elmore's point. Joshua Ramo (2016) makes a similar and more detailed argument that we are now entering a massively "connected world" that is requiring what he calls "a seventh sense," which is the ability to participate laterally and vertically in a massive interlay of global networking. We are willing to acknowledge that this phenomenon is rapidly ramifying and that it could blow apart schooling as we know it. We can only say that if this happens, our deep learners will be better equipped to deal with it. Indeed some of our deep learning leaders (including and perhaps especially the young ones) may lead networked learning systems in the future that become part of new learning that may not require schools as they are commonly thought of today.

A key component of any future will require new measures to assess both the shifting learning practices and their outcomes, to which we now turn.

Notes

_____

_____

_____

_____

_____

_____

_____

_____

_____

_____

_____

_____

_____

_____

_____

_____

_____

_____

_____

> " The goal of measurement is not only to do things right but to do the right things and continuously improve doing that. "

—PEARL ZHU

Chapter 9

NEW MEASURES FOR DEEP LEARNING

New Measures

The design, implementation, and assessment of learning depend always on our capacity to measure learners' progress and define their success. In our overall model, there are many components to assess and learn about. The main new domain to figure out is the 6Cs of global competencies (character, citizenship, collaboration, communication, creativity, and critical thinking) and the learning progressions that would best develop and measure them in practice. In this chapter, we focus on the measurement of the two core components of our model: the 6Cs and their realization in practice; and the four elements of deep learning design.

Throughout this book we have discussed deep learning as that which will prepare learners to drive their thinking, their lives, and the world forward. We have emphasized the deep learning competencies (6Cs) as crucial to students' capacity to flourish in the modern world. We stressed the importance of designing deep learning that supports students' development of these competencies, mastery of academic content, and capacity for applying and creating *meaningful* learning to make a real difference in lives and communities. This shift in values away from standardization and content memorization toward the creation and application of new and powerful knowledge and competencies necessitates a transformative shift in measurement tools and practices. The difference here is the difference between measuring what students know and measuring whether that knowledge, combined with key learning competencies, will prepare students to learn, create, act, and succeed.

> The design, implementation, and assessment of learning depend always on our capacity to measure learners' progress and define their success.

Deep Learning Competencies

The deep learning competencies (6Cs) are at the heart of what's critical for learners today. Measurement of students' deep learning competency development differs greatly from the types of assessment common in education systems globally. It requires not only an understanding of the competencies themselves, but also the capacity to connect that understanding with a wide range of learning evidence and to design learning that facilitates both the development and measurement of deep learning outcomes. In addition, deep learning can only develop when the right conditions are in place to foster its growth, supporting schools, clusters of schools, and systems to ensure that deep learning takes root and makes a real and lasting difference for students.

From the descriptions of what deep learning looks like with respect to each deep learning competency, we developed *Deep Learning Progressions* for each of the 6Cs designed to

- describe what learning looks like at each level of a fluid progression,

- provide a shared language and common understanding for developing and measuring deep learning outcomes, and

- measure and track student progress in developing each of the six deep learning competencies.

In the Deep Learning Progressions, each deep learning competency is broken into dimensions that combine to provide a complete picture of the skills, capabilities, and attitudes that contribute to success in the 6Cs (see Figure 9.1). For each dimension, they describe what learning looks like for students who display *limited*, *emerging*, *developing*, *accelerating*, or *proficient* evidence of development for that dimension. Teachers rate their students' level of development based on the descriptions provided and the wide range of evidence examined and synthesized.

Figure 9.1 • Collaboration Learning Progression

Collaboration Deep Learning Progression

Work interdependently and synergistically in teams with strong interpersonal and team-related skills including effective management of team dynamics and challenges, making substantive decisions together, and learning from and contributing to the learning of others.

Dimension	Limited Evidence	Emerging	Developing	Accelerating	Proficient
Working interdependently as a team	Learners either work individually on learning tasks or collaborate informally in pairs or groups but do not really work together as a team. Learners may discuss some issues or content together but skip over important substantive decisions (such as how the process will be managed), which has significant adverse impacts on how well the collaboration works.	Learners work together in pairs or groups and are responsible for completing a task for the group to achieve its work. At this level, tasks may not be well matched to each individual's strengths and expertise and group members' contributions may not be equitable. Learners are starting to make some decisions together but may still be leaving the most important substantive decisions to one or two members.	Learners decide together how to match tasks to the individual strengths and expertise of team members, and then work effectively together in pairs or groups. Learners involve all members in making joint decisions about an important issue, problem, or process and developing a team solution.	Learners can articulate how they work together in a way that is interdependent and uses each person's strengths in the best possible way to make sound substantive decisions and develop ideas and solutions. Interdependent teamwork is clearly evident in that learners' contributions are woven together to communicate an overarching idea and/or create a product.	Learners demonstrate a highly effective and synergistic approach to working interdependently in a way that not only leverages each member's strengths but also provides opportunities for each to build on those strengths and learn new skills. This includes ensuring that substantive decisions are discussed at a deep level that ensures each team member's strengths and perspectives are infused to come to the best possible decision that benefits all.
Interpersonal and team-related skills	Although learners may help each other on tasks that contribute to a joint work product or outcome, interpersonal and team-related skills are not yet evident. Learners do not yet demonstrate a genuine sense of empathy or a shared purpose for working together.	Learners report and demonstrate a sense of collective ownership of the work and show some interpersonal and team-related skills. The focus is on achieving a common or joint outcome, product, design, response, or decision, but at this level the key decisions may be taken or dominated by one or two members.	Learners demonstrate not only good interpersonal skills and collective ownership of the work, but an active sense of shared responsibility is also evident. From beginning to end, the team listens effectively, negotiates, and agrees on the goals, content, process, design, and conclusions of their work.	Learners can clearly articulate how joint responsibility for the work and its product or outcome pervades the entire task. Strong skills in listening, facilitation, and effective teamwork ensure that all voices are heard and reflected in the ways of working or work product.	Learners take an active responsibility, both individually and collectively, for ensuring that the collaborative process works as effectively as possible, that each person's ideas and expertise are used to maximum advantage, and that each work product or outcome is of the highest possible quality or value.

(Continued)

Figure 9.1 • (Continued)

Dimension	Limited Evidence	Emerging	Developing	Accelerating	Proficient
Social, emotional, and intercultural skills	Learners have a basic sense of awareness about themselves and how their behavior affects others. They tend to see things only from their own perspective. In some cases, this may inhibit their ability to form positive relationships.	Learners have a growing awareness of who they are, where they fit in the world, and how their behavior affects other people. This self-awareness is starting to provide a base for better understanding of how other people's emotions and viewpoints differ from their own.	Learners have good awareness of who they are and where their own perspective comes from. Self-awareness and listening skills allow them to better understand and empathize with the emotions and viewpoints of others, moving beyond "tolerance" or "acceptance" to genuinely valuing perspectives quite different from their own.	Learners have a strong sense of self and understand where their own perspective comes from and how it differs from others'. They listen carefully, empathize with the emotions and viewpoints of others, and use these to enrich their own learning. As a team member, they work effectively in ways that support, encourage, challenge, and grow not just themselves, but others as well.	Learners have highly developed social and emotional skills grounded in a clear sense of their individual and cultural identity. They communicate well across cultures and disciplines, work effectively in teams, and form positive relationships. The skills they have developed in perspective-taking and empathy, understanding someone else's perspective—and changing their behavior as a result—clearly enhance team functioning.
Leveraging digital	Although learners use some digital elements for the task, these were very "surface level" and did not substantially contribute to the quality or output of the collaboration.	Learners used digital opportunities to facilitate shared ways of working, in ways that could not have been done otherwise, although they are unlikely to have significantly deepened the collaborative process.	Learners used digital aspects effectively to encourage interdependent work, speed up feedback, accelerate innovation cycles, and deepen the nature of the collaboration among members.	Learners can clearly articulate how infusing a digital element has facilitated interdependence, deepened the nature of the collaboration, built a better sense of shared responsibility, and improved the team's ability to make substantive decisions together.	Learners used digital elements ubiquitously throughout the task in powerful ways to deepen the quality of collaboration and encourage innovation. Learners can articulate in detail about how each digital element has accelerated and enhanced the team's learning and can apply that understanding to new and different contexts.

Dimension	Limited Evidence	Emerging	Developing	Accelerating	Proficient
Managing team dynamics and challenges	Learners mishandle team challenges in one of two ways: (1) They get deeply invested in their own viewpoint, lack the empathy to hear or learn from others, and have difficulty suspending judgment to genuinely listen to others' views; or (2) They avoid conflict by deferring to others' views instead of sharing their own or will change their views quickly in the face of inappropriate peer pressure. As a result, the team gets stuck in conflict or may move forward in the wrong direction or one that the team does not share.	At this level, learners still need guidance to forge and maintain positive working relationships and to resist inappropriate peer pressure. They are starting to take a more considered approach to dealing with disagreements, asking each member to share their perspective, and discussing any differences. They are only just beginning to dig beneath those differences to identify what underpins them, which makes it difficult to resolve issues effectively and without unnecessary conflict.	Learners generally work quite effectively in a team, although they are likely to need help with conflict resolution, inappropriate peer pressure, and other challenging issues from time to time. They are developing the ability to identify what underpins their own and others' points of view. They are getting better at clearly and respectfully expressing their own viewpoints and listening to and learning from others. They still need to better pick their battles to ensure in-depth discussion on relatively minor issues doesn't hold up team progress.	Learners are more skilled at identifying what underpins their own and others' points of view. They pick their battles in deciding what to debate. They are building both courage and clarity to express their own viewpoints and listen to and learn from others. They are becoming skilled at exploring different opinions in ways that contribute to the learning of others without holding up team progress.	Learners have a deep understanding of what underpins their own and others' points of view, the courage and clarity to effectively express their own viewpoints, and the empathy to hear and learn from others. They respectfully explore different opinions in ways that enrich both their own and others' learning and thinking and allow the team to move forward in the direction that the team identifies.

Source: McEachen, J., & Quinn, J. *Collaboration Deep Learning Progression.* Copyright © 2014 by New Pedagogies for Deep Learning™ (NPDL)

Deep Learning Design

We discussed in Chapters 5 and 6 the four elements of deep learning design and how each must come together seamlessly in the design and implementation of deep learning experiences. Three tools assist this process:

1. The *New Pedagogies Learning Design Protocol* is used with the Collaborative Inquiry Cycle to support teachers in the design of deep learning experiences.

2. The *New Pedagogies Learning Design Rubric* describes what a deep learning experience looks like for each element of deep learning design at multiple stages of a fluid progression. It facilitates the assessment of deep learning experience design and supports deep learning experience redesigns.

3. The *Teacher Self-Assessment* supports teachers in identifying areas of strength and those in need of improvement in their design of deep learning experiences.

After teachers have designed, implemented, assessed, and reflected on a chosen deep learning experience, they have the opportunity to design and share *Deep Learning Exemplars*—examples of learning design, implementation, assessment, and outcomes that describe how deep learning develops and what it looks like in action. Exemplars are shared in the form of documents, written or visual descriptions and reflections, videos, pictures, or any other means of representing and describing the deep learning that occurred. Collectively, they describe what deep learning looks like at every level of the Deep Learning Progressions and facilitate collective identification of the new pedagogies that accelerate deep learning outcomes for students.

Due to the rich and expansive information provided in teachers' exemplars, they have emerged as a powerful tool in their own right, capable of demonstrating application of deep learning measures and tools and describing how teachers are finding success in developing deep learning outcomes.

Early Findings

The 6Cs

New Pedagogies for Deep Learning (NPDL) collects the New Measures data from participants on the *Deep Learning Hub*, a collaborative learning and data collection platform designed to support NPDL participants in their deep learning journey. All data is collected with the expectation that findings will be shared throughout the partnership to inform work with deep learning at the classroom, school, cluster, system, and global levels. In 2016, NPDL published its first Global Report, designed to provide a description of the global baseline level of deep learning as demonstrated by the words, work exemplars, and other submitted data of NPDL participants globally. In addition, the report highlighted early findings regarding the conditions consistent with deep learning development, methods for successful navigation of implementation challenges, and the early impact of deep learning for both students and educators (New Pedagogies for Deep Learning, 2016). Reports will be published annually to measure growth from this baseline and to further the impact of deep learning globally.

Although participants are still in the early stages of their work with the new measures, early findings regarding the deep learning competencies include the following:

> As a global baseline, students' level of development of the deep learning competencies . . . is widely *Emerging*; the way in which learning has been traditionally designed and implemented has not effectively developed deep learning outcomes. The measurement of students' deep learning progression has demonstrated the impact of NPDL tools and processes in developing the 6Cs. (NPDL, 2016, p. 1)

The collection of Deep Learning Progression ratings reveals a wealth of information on student and school outcomes. Along with ratings on each dimension of the Deep Learning Progressions, teachers also provide a rating for each student's overall development of a given competency. Figure 9.2 displays baseline overall ratings for each of the 6Cs at each level of the progression.

Across the 6Cs, over 50% of students were rated as demonstrating either *limited* or *emerging* evidence of each deep learning competency. As a baseline, the competencies on which students demonstrate the highest level of progression are *creativity* and *critical thinking*. Globally, participants have shared the profound impact of finally having a language to frame engagement with these competencies that before may have been at the surface level. The capacity to understand and talk deeply about creativity, for example, has enhanced teachers' design of learning experiences and structuring of learning environments in ways that maximize the learner's creative potential. Excitement around these new opportunities has seen creativity emerge as a "catalytic C" in that it supports students' capacity to develop other competencies in meaningful, creative ways. The complexity of measuring critical thinking is another competency that is discussed widely but not widely engaged in at a deep level. This has led participants to focus heavily on this competency from the outset to develop learners who can construct meaningful knowledge and apply it in the real world.

With the exception of *Citizenship*, all competencies show the greatest number of students rated at the *Emerging* level of the progression. Globally,

Figure 9.2 • Deep Learning Progression Ratings

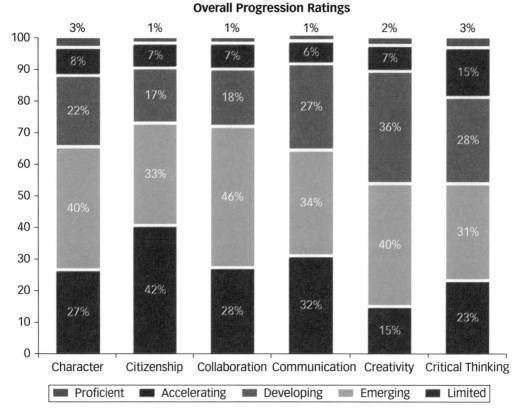

Source: Copyright © 2014 by New Pedagogies for Deep Learning™ (NPDL)

the *Citizenship* competency yielded the lowest baseline ratings, as 75% of rated students were at either the *Limited* or *Emerging* level, and 42% were rated as demonstrating *Limited* evidence of development. NPDL defines *citizenship* as thinking like global citizens, having compassion for others, considering global issues based on a deep understanding of diverse values and worldviews, and having a commitment and ability to solve ambiguous and complex real-world problems that impact human and environmental sustainability. Across the dimensions of the *citizenship* competency, students demonstrated the highest level of progress in their genuine interest in human and environmental sustainability and the lowest level of progression in their development of a global perspective. Issues that impact global sustainability and success are meaningful and interesting to the lives of learners throughout the world. Learning that nurtures this interest and helps students develop a global perspective will support them to understand and solve the issues that are meaningful to their own lives and the global community.

While citizenship is an emerging educational focus strengthened by increasing global connectedness and awareness, collaborative learning has long been a staple of education. However, the baseline overall ratings show that 74% of students demonstrate *limited* or *emerging* development of the *collaboration* competency, with 46% of students rated at the *emerging* level. Although students may collaborate on a regular basis, overall competence in collaborating *deeply* is still emerging. Proficient collaboration does not simply rely on the quality of a group's work product. It encompasses students' ability to manage team dynamics and challenges, make substantive group decisions, and learn from and contribute to the learning of others. As originally conceptualized, traditional teaching and learning processes have not developed deep learning outcomes, which instead require learning experiences deepened by the new pedagogies.

The following case examines findings from one group of NPDL schools, which measured students' competency development at multiple points in the learning process to track students' progress in developing deep learning outcomes.

The growth in Region A, experienced over less than a full year's involvement with NPDL, reflects the effect of learning in the new pedagogies on the development of the competencies students need for success.

This effect is clearly demonstrated in teachers' design and sharing of deep learning experiences, which we turn to here in our discussion of the new pedagogies.

Case: Deep Learning Progression

Now that baseline data has been collected, NPDL will look to measure overall movement with regard to the baseline, as well as individual learner progression at multiple points in their learning process. While almost all data collected to this point measures a single point in students' level of progression, teachers from one group of NPDL schools (referred to here as "Region A") rated their learners' deep learning progression from the beginning of their journey with deep learning to the end of their first academic year following NPDL's introduction.

Of the 157 student ratings across each of the 6Cs, over 73% demonstrate progression in deep learning competency development, with over 21% of student ratings measuring two or more levels of progression. Students with ratings for *citizenship*, the competency for which learners' baseline level of development is the most widely limited globally, experienced significant growth in their development of the competency. Of the 46 students with yearlong data, over 93% advanced along the *citizenship* Deep Learning Progression, with over 37% progressing multiple levels.

The New Pedagogies

The four elements of deep learning design—pedagogical practices, partnerships, learning environments, and leveraging digital—have been emphasized by participants throughout NPDL as pivotal to teachers' capacity to embed new pedagogies in their design of deep learning experiences.

Evidence collected from teachers' Deep Learning Exemplars reveals key learning across each element (see Figure 9.3).

Figure 9.3 • Deep Learning Exemplar Evidence

Pedagogical Practices	Learning Partnerships
• Common elements of new pedagogies learning design include: co-design by students, teachers, families, and community members; student reflection on their growth and learning at multiple points in the learning process, using peer and other feedback along with success criteria set for and by the group; and cross-curricular learning that connects to and makes a difference in the lives of students and the world. • Teachers are finding success designing deep learning experiences that develop the deep learning competencies *and* support a variety of other developmental focuses (see later).	• Learning partnerships between students are cultivated in the new pedagogies, leading to improved collaboration and knowledge sharing within classes and between grade levels. • Student agency has been strengthened by new relationships in which students and teachers are partners in the design, implementation, and measurement of learning. • Partnering with parents, families, and members of the community has strengthened learning outcomes and student engagement and resulted in learning for all involved.
Learning Environments	**Leveraging Digital**
• When given ownership of their learning, students develop and reveal their capabilities in ways previously unavailable to them and gravitate toward learning that has a positive impact on their own and others' lives. • Deep learning facilitates knowledge and competency development anytime and anywhere, because students' learning is led beyond classroom walls where it is further cultivated by their families and members of the community. • Cultures of learning, innovation, and reflection empower all their members to take risks, reflect on and learn from successes and challenges, and contemplate every action and decision in light of the impact it will have on learning outcomes.	• Technology is an *enabler* and *accelerator* of deep learning—teaching in the new pedagogies is the true *driver* of deep learning outcomes for all learners. • Focus is best placed not on the sophistication or complexity of the technologies themselves, but rather on how they can be *leveraged* to deepen learning experiences. • Effective leveraging of digital technologies enhances all other elements of new pedagogies learning design: It facilitates deep learning partnerships with students and community experts regardless of geographical location; enables a wealth of opportunities for learning design and implementation; and supports students' capacity to take control of their learning both within and outside classroom walls.

Source: Copyright © 2014 by New Pedagogies for Deep Learning™ (NPDL)

The design of deep learning experiences not only develops deep learning outcomes but also does so through supporting teachers in areas identified throughout NPDL as developmental focuses, such as (1) using the Deep Learning Progressions alongside a broad range of evidence to measure deep learning, and (2) linking deep learning and the curriculum.

Assessment Evidence for Measuring Deep Learning

In their descriptions of deep learning experiences, submitted in the form of Deep Learning Exemplars, teachers often included both information on the assessments used throughout the experience as well as pre- and post-experience Progression ratings.

In an example from the NPDL Australia Cluster, students at Brauer College engaged in a deep learning experience in which they worked collaboratively to design a Rube Goldberg machine. Assessment approaches used included the following:

- Students completed a Self-Assessment Sheet to evaluate their social and cognitive collaboration skills.

- Using Padlet, students shared what they already knew about collaboration and how it differs from group work.

- Video footage of progress.

- Peer contributions to student designs through observation.

- Using Google Docs alongside Solution Fluency, a six-step process designed to help students stay on track.

- Assessment rubric used both by teachers and students.

- Individual and group reflections task.

- NPDL Collaboration Deep Learning Progression.

- Student self-assessment using a student version of the Collaboration Deep Learning Progression.

- Student voting on the most creative and innovative Rube Goldberg machine.

This and other Deep Learning Exemplars demonstrate the extent to which deep learning experiences support teachers to use a wide range of assessments and approaches to better understand student performance and measure deep learning.

The following graphics from an Exemplar from the NPDL Canada Cluster (see Figures 9.4 and 9.5) show how evidence from a deep learning experience is used alongside the *citizenship* Progression to measure a learner's growth on one dimension of the competency (A Global Perspective). The exemplar by teacher Kerri Denyes of Stirling Public School is titled "An Adventure With Air and Water."

Figure 9.4 • Pre-Experience Exemplar

Marker Students—Pre-Assessment

Highlight which C is being assessed:

☐ CREATIVITY   ☐ CRITICAL THINKING
☐ COMMUNICATION   ☐ CHARACTER
☑ CITIZENSHIP   ☐ COLLABORATION

SCORING: 1—Limited evidence 2— Emerging 3—Developing 4—Accelerating 5—Proficient

Student Name/ Identifier	Male/ Female	Student Pre-rating	A Global Perspective
927252035	F	2	• Shared with the group her family's involvement with global issues (purchasing chickens for a family in Africa at Christmas). She understood the global connection but did not seem to have a concrete understanding of larger implications for these actions.
927252036	M	1	• Made connections to his own personal experiences (e.g., Earth Rangers), which inspired others' to contribute to the conversation. His initial connections were not deeply rooted to an understanding of world issues but did prompt some further conversation about world issues.

Source: Denyes, K. (2016). An Adventure With Air and Water [NPDL Exemplar].

Figure 9.5 • Post-Experience Exemplar

Marker Students—Post

Highlight which C is being assessed:

☐ CREATIVITY   ☐ CRITICAL THINKING
☐ COMMUNICATION   ☐ CHARACTER
☑ CITIZENSHIP   ☐ COLLABORATION

SCORING: 1—Limited evidence 2—Emerging 3—Developing 4—Accelerating 5—Proficient

Student Name/ Identifier	Male/ Female	Student Pre-rating	A Global Perspective
927252036	M	4	• Made connections between experiences and greater picture by identifying with global occurrences and sharing news stories that connected to our learning (e.g., warming climate and the effect on polar ice caps). • Asked questions that demonstrated deep thinking and extended conversations for our class. • Provided answers to questions posed in class that he had followed up with independently. • Brought the learning home (encouraged his family to change habits that would have an impact on the Earth).

Source: Denyes, K. (2016). An Adventure With Air and Water [NPDL Exemplar].

Linking Deep Learning and Curriculum

One of the major points of emphasis and reflection in early work with deep learning regards the linking or alignment of deep learning concepts and processes with local and national curriculum. It is the case that recent state or national curricula have begun to position global competencies as central to their priorities: the Australian state of Victoria; British Columbia, Canada; Finland; Ontario, Canada; and New Zealand, to name a few. These new curriculum documents do not have much to say about how to implement the competencies, nor for that matter how to assess them. This is where NPDL comes in. NPDL participants have commented on how the focus and tools of NPDL help them form the link to these new state curriculum documents and aspirations. In other words, deep learning works not against, but rather with and for new curriculum priorities. Let's take two examples from Canada and Finland.

The graphics in Figure 9.6, pulled from a Deep Learning Exemplar from Canada, show direct links to explicit curriculum focuses covering a range of curriculum areas. The numerical or alphabetical figures used below represent the contents of the country's own curriculum documents, identifying how they intend to address the requirements of the curriculum in alignment with the competencies.

Figure 9.6 • Exemplar: What Makes a Great Community, Millgrove Public School, Canada, Teacher: Jodie Howcroft

Collaborative Inquiry Reflections – Measure, Reflect, Change

Links to Curriculum:

Social Studies

People and Environments: The Local Community (Grade 1)

B2 Use the social studies inquiry process to investigate some aspects of the interrelationship between people and different natural and built features of their local community, with a focus on significant short- and long-term effects of this interrelationship

Global Communities (Grade 2)

B2 Use the social studies inquiry process to investigate aspects of the interrelationship between the natural environment, including the climate, of selected communities and the ways in which people in those communities live

Science

Understanding Life Systems – Needs and Characteristics of Living Things (Grade 1)

1.0 Assess the role of humans in maintaining a healthy environment

Understanding Life Systems – Growth and Changes in Animals (Grade 2)

1.0 Assess ways in which animals have an impact on society and the environment, and ways in which humans have an impact upon animals and the places where they live

(Continued)

Figure 9.6 • (Continued)

Understanding Earth and Space Systems – Air and Water in the Environment

1.0 Assess ways in which the actions of humans have an impact on the quality of air and water, and ways in which the quality of air and water has an impact on living things

Mathematics

Geometry and Spatial Sense

- describe the relative locations of objects using positional language (Grade 1)

- describe and represent the relative locations of objects, and represent objects on a map (Grade 2)

Collaborative Inquiry Reflections – Measure, Reflect, Change

Links to Curriculum:

Language

Writing (Grades 1 and 2)

2.1 Write short texts using a few simple forms

2.5 Begin to identify, with support and direction, their point of view and one possible different point of view about the topic

Reading (Grades 1 and 2)

1.1 Read a few different types of literary texts, graphic texts *(e.g., environmental print, signs),* and informational texts

1.5 Use stated and implied information and ideas in texts, initially with support and direction, to make simple inferences and reasonable predictions about them

1.6 Extend understanding of texts by connecting the ideas in them to their own knowledge and experience, to other familiar texts, and to the world around them

Oral Communications (Grades 1 and 2)

2.2 Demonstrate an understanding of appropriate speaking behaviour in a variety of situations, including paired sharing and small- and large-group discussions

Health

Personal Safety and Injury Prevention (Grade 1)

C3.1 Demonstrate an understanding of how to stay safe and avoid injuries to themselves and others in a variety of situations, using knowledge about potential risks at home, in the community, and outdoors

Personal Safety and Injury Prevention (Grade 2)

C1.1 Demonstrate an understanding of practices that enhance personal safety in the home

---

Source: Howcroft, J. (2016). What Makes a Great Community? [NPDL Exemplar].

A second example comes from the new national curriculum in Finland (see Figure 9.7). NPDL leaders in Finland mapped assessments against each curriculum area of focus, in relation to how they would develop key dimensions of the *character, collaboration,* and *communication* competencies.

In this example, the leveraging of digital technologies provides opportunities for seamless cross-curricular learning that facilitates collaborative learning among both students and teachers.

Figure 9.7 • **Leveraging Digital and the Arts, Kiviniemi Primary School, Oulu, Finland, Teachers: Anne-Marie Ilo and Maarit Saarenkunnas**

Subtasks: An Outline				
One color represents one task, which creates a continuum from one school subject to another.				
ICT and Art	**Finnish Language**	**English Language**	**Geography**	**Learning to Learn, Thinking Skills, Social Skills**
Filming and editing an interview	Writing a script for the interview	Collaboratively created question pool	Interview video	Finding one's strengths and using them in school work
Collaborative work in OneNote	Collaborative work in OneNote	Writing a script for the interview	Collaborative work in OneNote	Finding an active role in school work
Visual presentation (PowerPoint)	Oral presentation	Interview video	Presentations (oral and written)	Finding joy in working
Information searches		Written and a video presentations of a character	Video presentations of a character	Learning planning and tenacity
Symmetry drawing			Collecting information from the work of peers on information sheets	Learning to work on collaboration and communication skills
			Activity book and notebook tasks	Practicing self- and peer evaluation

Source: Ilo, A., & Saarenkunnas, M. (2016). Europe [NPDL Exemplar].

The language of the New Measures, in addition to providing a shared understanding within the context of individual countries and schools, was kept sufficiently broad to allow for implementation on a global scale. The adaptability of the New Measures supports participants to first determine what is important in their individual context and then to design a pathway forward. For many schools, this model has required a change in thinking and practice across the clusters of schools implementing deep learning, because participants in the past have been exposed predominantly to step-by-step implementation processes affording limited room for adaptability and contextualization. The fact that at the outset of work with deep

The adaptability of the New Measures supports participants to first determine what is important in their individual context and then to design a pathway forward.

learning best practices and approaches were altogether unknown necessitated an exploratory partnership design reliant on participants' willingness to create, learn from their approach, and share that learning within and across clusters. This sharing of learning is taking shape and making a difference for learners, teachers, and other leaders, as we explore further in the following section.

Work with deep learning thus far has demonstrated that global deep learning implementation is not only possible but also making a significant difference for learners and educators regardless of their education system. The success of NPDL's global implementation speaks directly to the interpretability and adaptability of its tools and processes. Participants are successfully implementing the framework within *and to meet* a strikingly broad range of system and curriculum expectations. The evidence collected throughout the beginning stages of this journey has proven the viability of a global framework for deep learning, which will continue to strengthen as participant experiences further inform initiative design and direction.

The Global Moderation Process

We've discussed the importance of Deep Learning Exemplars in providing opportunities for teachers to describe their work as well as the deep learning outcomes that develop as a result. By sharing their own and engaging with others' exemplars, each participant would have the opportunity to play a critical role in developing deep learning outcomes on a global scale. What was needed was a process for sharing, measuring, and building on the learning experiences described in the exemplars to identify and further develop the new pedagogies that best facilitate deep learning.

The level of learning experienced by moderation participants sheds light on the importance of the moderation process for establishing inter-rater reliability, as well as its impact on learning at all levels of the initiative. Globally, it reveals the need for a high level of emphasis on deep learning design and exemplar moderation, so as to provide participants with the most powerful examples of deep learning for their own continued growth and development.

Other key points of learning identified through the process of moderation include the following:

- For each learning experience, no matter the size and scope, teachers can use the New Measures to think about how specific elements can be deepened to improve outcomes for learners.

- Learning is deepest when it connects to students' lives—who they are, how they fit into the world, and how they can contribute back. No matter the learning goal, teachers have the opportunity to think about how otherwise ordinary learning can be deepened to make a difference in students' lives and the world.

- Results of global moderation identified *Leveraging Digital* as the element most in need of improvement globally. When accelerating learner outcomes through digital technologies, the focus should be placed on how the tools are *directly facilitating* student engagement with the curriculum and development of the 6Cs.

Final Thoughts

We have demonstrated that deep learning is already taking hold in K–12 education systems throughout the world. Primary and secondary schools are giving weight to new measures of deep learning and using them alongside a broad mix of assessment evidence to develop a complete picture of individual students' success.

One of the major challenges facing a widespread shift toward deep learning involves moving beyond primary and secondary schools to form a link with higher education (Scott, 2016; Tijssen & Yegros, 2016). It's easier to compare students on test scores and other standardized measures than it is to leverage a wide range of evidence about who students are, what they have done and are capable of outside their test scores, and how they hope to contribute to the lives of others and the world. The key question concerns how to look beyond single indicators of student success and potential to focus on and understand what really matters. The admissions process isn't more equitable when students have the same small number of opportunities to demonstrate their learning, but instead when they have the opportunity to showcase their learning in diverse and wide-ranging ways.

Deep learning provides this opportunity. As stated by one NPDL leader:

> [With deep learning] students get to be smart and good in different ways, and traditional school doesn't always provide them with those opportunities. NPDL gives all kids the chance to be amazing and show the gifts they bring. The way we view our students is changing along with the opportunities we give them to be great.

In short, one of the next frontiers in deep learning is to link secondary school developments to new pedagogies and assessment in the postsecondary sector, but that would be the subject of another book.

Returning to the measurement process outlined in the beginning of this chapter, our next step involves using the learning gained through work with the New Measures to better focus capacity building efforts and adjust tools and processes as necessary. The learning detailed in this chapter has informed and will continue to inform next steps with deep learning.

CHAPTER 9

The New Measures were created with the goal that after being sufficiently tested in education systems in different countries, the partnership would come together to assess and revise the tools in light of the learning that occurred. We are now refining the New Measures of deep learning to improve their capacity building and measurement capacities, along with their impact in developing deep learning outcomes.

As part of the bigger picture, there is the necessity of assessing the 6Cs as learning outcomes—competencies that deep learning graduates, so to speak, would possess. We have an agreement with OECD to help work on its development of Global Competencies—ones that overlap considerably with our work. Agreeing on how to define global competencies internationally is quite complex, as countries attribute different meanings to the same terms. We feel our approach to assessing learning progressions will feed positively into these global debates. As we all move forward, it is essential that the focus be on the conditions and processes of accomplishing deep learning in practice—the subject of this book—as well as the outcomes themselves. We look forward to participating in these developments as they unfold.

Finally, and fundamentally, *engage the world change the world* is deeply spiritual. All religions and all human secular values find a foundational place in deep learning. Acting upon the world to learn about it while transforming it and yourself toward continuous fulfillment is both evolutionary and heavenly.

SECTION III
A Precarious Future

" In Greek mythology were three dangerous mermaid-like creatures who lured nearby sailors with their enchanting music and voices to shipwreck on the rocky coast of their island. "

Chapter 10

SIRENS OR SALVATION

Deep Learning Hell or Heaven

The Sirens

We doubt if there has ever been a time when humankind as a whole was so aware of the dangers and opportunities that abound, and so ambivalent about what to do about it, and about the possible outcomes. If there was ever the need to heed Paulo Freire's (2000) advice about the role of education, it is now: "Act upon and transform the world [in order to] move towards ever new possibilities of a fuller and richer life individually and collectively" (p. 32). This is as good a definition of the purpose of deep learning as any.

In this final chapter we have two big issues to address. What is the difference between deep learning hell and heaven? And the big one—deep learning's ultimate challenge: addressing growing inequality in society.

Getting to Deep Learning Hell or Heaven

Our colleague, sociologist Jal Mehta, received a grant to study examples of deep learning in secondary schools across the United States. He and his team visited schools identified as engaging in deep learning. Months later he reported that sadly they found hardly any examples of what would constitute authentic deep learning (Mehta & Fine, 2015). He then set out his interpretation in a blog that he titled "Deeper Learning: 10 Ways You Can Die" (Mehta & Fine, 2016).

Jal basically said that the status quo is blocking deep learning even among those who claim to be doing it. What he found was the allure of sirens: sounds great until you get there. Our experience was different because we explicitly framed what deep learning would look like and built an infrastructure of people and tools to enable it in practice and to learn from each other's experience. Let's compare Mehta's 10 ways you can die with our 10 ways to get to deep learning heaven.

Putting deep learning into practice is much more challenging than people thought because it involves innovation, new relationships, and discovering things you didn't know before. It requires engaging scores of students who

10 Ways to Die With Deep Learning

1. If you haven't experienced deep or powerful learning yourself
2. If you are unwilling to reimagine the "grammar" of schooling.
3. If you don't respect your students in the present as opposed to the future
4. If you don't give students some choice
5. If you don't live by "less is more"
6. If you aren't willing to admit you don't know the answer
7. If you don't normalize failure and create opportunities for revision and improvement
8. If you don't help students feel like they belong in your class or in your domain
9. If you aren't willing to set the world a little askew
10. If you don't realize that creating deeper learning is a countercultural enterprise

10 Ways to Get to Deep Learning Heaven

1. Going from simple to complex ideas
2. Learning that is simultaneously personal and collective
3. Learning that changes relationships and pedagogy
4. Learning that sticks
5. Learning that involves a critical mass of others
6. Learning built on innovation relative to key problems and issues
7. Learning that attacks inequity to get excellence for all
8. Learning that engages the world to change the world
9. Learning that creates citizens of tomorrow today
10. Learning where young people make older people better

are often alienated from school. It must stare down the conservatism of the status quo.

We said earlier that no country or state has developed the policy infrastructure to enable deep learning across the system. Many of the teachers, principals, and district leaders in NPDL were challenged by systemic barriers to implementing deep learning (such as assessment systems, report cards, and curriculum coverage). We note that several jurisdictions (for example, Finland, British Columbia) recently announced new curriculum policies favorable to deep learning. While there are limited ideas about how to go about implementation in these new domains, this may be changing.

In September 2017, Ontario made a bold policy move in the direction of state framing and support for deep learning. In addition to a new and explicit *Equity Action Plan*, the province established an external team to review existing assessment practices as conducted by the Education and Quality Assessment Office (EQAO), and committed to conducting a "refresh" of curriculum, including math and other subjects. Most interesting, the province called for a new report card based on six transferable skills (or global competencies): critical thinking, innovation and creativity, self-directed learning, collaboration, communication, and citizenship. These are, of course, the 6Cs, with "character" being replaced by "self-directed learning."

Other governments are moving in a similar direction. In October 2017, New Zealand announced policy changes abolishing National Standards in favor of a new system that utilizes learning progressions and other elements compatible with deep learning and the 6Cs. It is noteworthy that New Zealand and Ontario's changes remove or reduce systemic barriers to deep learning such as criteria related to assessing learning outcomes.

These developments are not establishing a systematic policy infrastructure, but they are indicative of what we predict will be a strong move in this direction across the world. Deep learning is contagious upward to policy makers as well as laterally at the grass roots level.

The Plot Thickens

Making progress on deep learning is becoming more difficult because of two external factors: dramatically growing inequality, especially in the United States, and a digital future that is making Moore's law (the number of transistors in an integrated circuit will double every 2 years; 1965) look conservative.

Urban expert Richard Florida (2017) recently completed a study of cities in the United States and documented what he called *The Urban Crisis*. Florida documents what he calls "the widening gap between the relatively advantaged group, and just about everyone else" (pp. 55–56). Accompanying this trend is the consolidation of intergeneration poverty: "Two-thirds of African Americans who were raised in the poorest 25 percent of America neighborhoods are raising their own children in similarly disadvantaged neighborhoods" (p. 117).

> Attacking inequity with excellence, combined with community investments, can lift people out of endless cycles of failure.

These developments give special urgency to our equity hypothesis, namely that attacking inequity with excellence, combined with community investments, can lift people out of endless cycles of failure. On a small scale, we see this in Lynwood School District—a school system of 15,000 high poverty students adjacent to Compton in Los Angeles that raised its graduation rates above 90% (12% above the state average) by focusing on a combination of nonacademic needs in health and housing and excellence of learning within the school. Richard Florida (2017) names seven pillars of a coordinated solution, one of which is "tackle poverty by investing in people and places." Students like those in Lynwood are our hidden figures, capable of doing well through the combined support of health, housing, safety, and schooling.

In short, we need to combine and integrate community development and good schools. Once we get to deep learning for all, it is not just a matter of reducing inequality; it also includes prosperity of all. How much good can hordes of young people do who are skilled in the 6Cs (character, citizenship, collaboration, communication, creativity, and critical thinking)? Reduce inequality through the excellence of deep learning for all children and watch societal health grow.

Harnessing our digital future, as McAfee and Brynjolfsson (2017) put it, is another matter. Critical reasons for developing deep learning capacities keep piling on as if it were a conspiracy to make humans better (or destroy them). McAfee and Brynjolfsson analyze the explosive and interactive development of *machines, platforms, and crowds.* Machines consist of the expansive capabilities of digital creations; platforms involve the organization and distribution of information; and crowds refer to "the startlingly large amount of human knowledge, expertise, and enthusiasm distributed all over the world and now available, and able to be focused, online" (p. 14). The authors then couple the three forces into pairs: "minds and machines, products and platforms, the core [existing knowledge, and capabilities] and the crowd" (p. 18). They suggest that successful enterprises will be those that integrate and leverage the new triadic set to do things very differently than what we do today. Complex to say the least—and we are not even going to call in the robots!

Now to the point:

> Those that don't undertake this [new] work, and stick closely to today's technological and organizational status quo, will be making essentially the same choice as those that stuck with steam power. . . . And eventually, they'll meet the same fate. (McAfee & Brynjolfsson, 2017, p. 24)

To us this legitimizes, and indeed projects into the unknown, just about everything we have been saying about deep learning. It blows open the "hidden figures" door relative to the equity hypothesis, shakes the foundation of regular schooling, and invites the expansion of deep learning as we have defined it. And, yes, it may mean that Elmore (2016) is correct: that the institution of schooling, as we know it, cannot possibly survive under the new conditions. We still say that schools, students, parents and other caregivers, and educators are well advised to get a head start on this "future unknown" by developing their global competencies, and by getting busy changing their worlds for the better.

Let's take a simple but dramatic example of exposing the hidden figures phenomenon. McAfee and Brynjolfsson tell us about Broward County, Florida, where identifying gifted children used to be by nomination by their parents and teachers. Most students in Broward were minorities, but 56% of the children in gifted programs were White. The district shifted to a method based on objective criteria: They gave every child in the district a nonverbal IQ test. "The result of this one change, as documented by economists David Card, and Laura Giuliano, were striking: 80% more African American and 130% more Hispanic students were identified as gifted" (McAfee & Brynjolfsson, 2017, p. 40).

Relying more on machines, platforms, and crowds reduces human bias. Put another way, the 6Cs are essential for the human connections in a digitized world that will be required to get things done. Our deep learning model, to use McAfee and Brynjolfsson's (2017) words, enables our learners to access and interact with the "crowd":

> As interconnected computing power has spread around the world and useful platforms have been built on top of it, the crowd has become a demonstrably viable and valuable resource. (p. 259)

Do we still need schools or something like them?

If schools can be beaten by a technology-enabled crowd, do we still need them? We cannot say that schools in their present form are required, but we are confident that our examination of deep learning points to what we do need, namely, learners skilled at the 6Cs who are organized and coordinated in some fashion.

Our additional and compatible reason for coordination, and the ultimate conclusion of our book, is that humans want and need each other. There is enough neuro-scientific evidence to conclude that humans are a social species. Their capacity to develop socially gets amplified or deadened depending on their life experience, and this makes a world of a difference for individuals and for the group.

In any case, the future is precarious and unknown. We like the image of the present that the giant and rapidly growing Chinese Internet company, Tencent, identifies as "being born in the wild" ("The Internet Challenge," 2015). It's a great metaphor for a rich and volatile environment of the kind we now have. For all intents and purposes, our learners coming into the world these days might as well be seen as being born in the wild because they will need all the wits and wisdom they can muster and be helped to muster. They will need the 6Cs and the assumption that the world is mysterious, dangerous, wondrous, and, to put it oddly, in need of help.

Not as farfetched as it sounds. As we fostered the 6Cs and deep learning in our global partnership, we experienced six *emerging discoveries*. It turns out that they are squarely in the domain of engage the world change the world.

As we do this work, we see cut across themes occurring spontaneously: *engage the world change the world; do good, learn more;* and *the world needs me.* Because these themes emerge from experiential deep learning, they are not superficial and Pollyannaish refrains. Our emerging discoveries are born

Engage the world change the world; do good, learn more; and the world needs me.

> ## Discoveries That Emerged When Implementing Deep Learning
>
> 1. *Helping humanity.* Children and youth have a natural affinity to improving humanity.
>
> 2. *Life and learning merge.* Learning is most powerful when it is closest to what is important in daily life. Personal purpose and making something worthwhile rules.
>
> 3. *Working with others is an intrinsic motivator.* Doing something of value with others is a deeply human experience.
>
> 4. *Character, citizenship, and creativity are catalytic Cs.* These are the drivers of comprehensive action to discover and make valuable things happen.
>
> 5. *Young people are the best change agents.* Babies onward, but not in isolation. Young and older people need each other: discover the synergy.
>
> 6. *Attack inequity with excellence.* As the world gets more unequal, the reverse power of deep learning to achieve greater excellence across the board becomes crucial for the survival of the planet.

Our best hope collectively is that deep learners inherit the world.

from deep learners at work. They occur in relation to the anxiety and the realization that machines, platforms, and the crowd will interact in unpredictable ways. In the face of these more powerful forces, the more essential will be the human capacity to connect and care. In a word, the more we will need deep learning as we have portrayed it.

Never has it been more crucial to have alert learners working in groups, plugged into the big picture. It could go horribly wrong, but we know that under all circumstances people will be better off if they are learners equipped with the 6Cs. Our best hope collectively is that deep learners inherit the world.

Appendix

THE SEVEN COUNTRIES

Catch a glimpse of the journey toward deep learning in each of our seven countries. No two countries are alike—some have a small number of schools, and others have hundreds. The book captures a range of just a few examples, but there are hundreds more rapidly emerging. The common language anchored by the 6Cs (character, citizenship, collaboration, communication, creativity, and critical thinking) allows teachers, leaders, and students to connect with deep understanding almost instantly. This is the power of positive contagion in action as deep learning becomes a momentum maker. Visit our website, **www.npdl.global,** to see more examples and follow the exciting journey.

Australia

In Australia, the Department of Education and Training for the state of Victoria and Tasmania took up the leadership role and began initially with 80 schools from Victoria State and 20 from Tasmania. In 2015, eight schools from Queensland joined as a sub cluster and within

©iStockphoto.com/cnythzl

a year expanded to 29. Australia moved to action rapidly by utilizing the comprehensive global suite of tools and processes but drove it internally with a strong capacity building approach that was tailored to the local needs. They developed extensive support structures and resources that were shared with, and highly valued by, the other countries. Collaborative inquiry was used as a deliberate mechanism to foster deep dialogue across all schools for the cross fertilization of ideas and skills.

Canada

Canada is organized into school boards under the jurisdiction of 10 provincial and 3 territorial Ministries of Education. There is no federal involvement or national curriculum, but the provinces engage frequently to ensure alignment across the country. Canada joined

©iStockphoto.com/alexsl

New Pedagogies for Deep Learning (NPDL) with 14 school boards and approximately 100 schools in 2014. Initially, schools were in two provinces: Ontario and Manitoba. Currently 28 district school boards, across six provinces, representing more than 300 schools, are actively engaged in NPDL. The geographically diverse school boards use virtual meetings regularly to share resources, investigate problems of practice, and moderate exemplars. Districts have robust capacity building approaches and value the ability to go outside to get better inside through the deep learning labs and cross-district visitations.

Finland

©iStockphoto.com/
claudiodivizia

Finland has been at the top of the OECD ratings for the past decade and hosts thousands of educators annually who want to learn their secret for student success. Despite the strong performance on international testing and the satisfaction of parents and community, the government set out to create a new national curriculum to prepare students for the digital world. At the same time this was being developed, a local partner, Microsoft, stepped forward to support a cluster of 100 schools to lead the way in deep learning. Finland began with a *whole system mindset* that NPDL would give them the "how to" that was missing in the new curriculum. They utilized the suite of tools to give precision and focus to planning and dialogue about implementing the new curriculum across municipalities. Finally, the collaborative inquiry and global moderation process were highly impactful in comparing their approach to what was possible in other global contexts. Organizationally, education is managed by municipalities. A single capacity building provider is connecting the 26 municipalities and over 250 schools in the deep learning work.

Netherlands

©iStockphoto.com/
flowgraph

The Netherlands has a unique context both organizationally and politically. It is committed to choice in education, which means anyone can open a school based on their personal beliefs, provided they meet Dutch education system standards. In response to societal demands for rapid changes in education, the Netherlands Ministry of Education, Culture and Science has invited a variety of partners to create a clear vision of how education will look in 2035. Participation in NPDL contributes directly to the national focus on transforming learning for modern and future education and invites participants to step outside their comfort zones and discover new, creative ways to optimize their own and others' practices. A capacity building organization has been crucial in connecting the diverse school boards on a common learning journey. A strong *capacity building* approach combined with the comprehensive tools has forged connections across schools that are *going outside to get better inside*. They describe the changes in the teaching process and the relationships with students as unthinkable even a year ago.

New Zealand

In October 2017, the recently elected government announced a policy change that abolished National Standards in favor of working with sector experts and practitioners on a new system that utilizes learning progressions and other elements compatible with deep learn-

©iStockphoto.com/alexsl

ing and the 6Cs. They look to strengthen public schooling by providing opportunities for schools to collaboratively design joint plans that utilize the process of the previous Communities of Learning (CoL). New Zealand continues its strong focus on successful programs to lift Māori achievement and is investigating the possibility of creating unique secondary school qualifications for Māori. They join the global challenge of designing assessment for deep learning by reviewing the ways of measuring competency success. The invitation to participate in the NPDL program aligns with their competency-based framework for curriculum. The schools saw NPDL's emphasis on the 6Cs and the development of new learning strategies and organizational structures as providing an ideal context for teachers and schools to collaborate in pursuing local and national goals. Starting with 7 schools, they expanded to 29 by using a strong capacity building approach, the moderation process, and *going outside to get better inside* by connecting across schools. It is noteworthy that the recent New Zealand policy changes are similar to those just announced in Ontario in that they remove or reduce systemic barriers (such as criteria for success) in favor of deep learning.

United States

The United States is vast and complex with varied local contexts and political structures. Four states have recently joined NPDL and are forming a virtual network to help them learn across geographic boundaries. California, Michigan, and Washington have been active for a year. Connecticut has an associate cluster.

©iStockphoto.com/
MargaretClavell

In all cases, the context, geography, and demographics are diverse, yet what pulls them in is the opportunity to learn with others inside their state but also interstate and globally. Several other states are organizing to join the partnership. They have used a strong face-to-face capacity building approach in each state, augmented by the virtual resources and connections.

Uruguay

©iStockphoto.com/
Viktorcvetkovic

Context matters, and the system example from Uruguay represents an aspiration to shift a whole country using a *go slow to go fast* strategy. Uruguay is a democracy that identified education as a crucial foundation for the future success of its population and set out 10 years ago to make a significant change from a highly centralized system to one that would tap into the potential of all. Ceibal, a government-funded but independent agency, has been fundamental in building capacity linked to technology. They used the suite of tools and processes as a touchstone to build common language and skills with the initial 100 schools. In Years 2 and 3, they developed more comprehensive and sustained approaches founded on their strong technology base and expanded to build capacity and touch more than 400 schools.

References

American Institutes of Research. (2014). *Study of deeper learning: Opportunities and outcomes*. Palo Alto, CA: Author.

Biggs, J., & Collis, K. (1982). *Evaluating the quality of learning: The SOLO taxonomy (structure of the observed learning outcome)*. New York, NY: Academic Press.

Cadwell, L. B. (1997). *Bringing Reggio Emilia home: An innovative approach to early childhood education*. New York, NY: Teachers College.

Cadwell, L. B. (2002). *Bringing learning to life: A Reggio approach to early childhood education*. New York, NY: Teachers College.

Clinton, J. (2013). The power of positive adult relationships: Connection is the key. Retrieved from http://www.edu.gov.on.ca/childcare/Clinton.pdf

Comber, B. (2013). Schools as meeting places: Critical and inclusive literacies in changing local environments. *Language Arts, 90*, 361–371.

Connection through relationship: The key to mental health. (2017, June 13). [Seminar]. Toronto, Canada.

Davidson, E. J., & McEachen, J. (2014). *Making the important measurable: Not the measurable important*. Seattle, WA: The Learner First.

The Deming Institute. (n.d.). The Deming system of profound knowledge. Retrieved from https://deming.org/explore/so-p-k

The Economist. (2017). Together, technology and teachers can revamp schools. Retrieved from https://www.economist.com/news/leaders/21725313-how-science-learning-can-get-best-out-edtech-together-technology-and-teachers-can

Elmore, R. (2016). Getting to scale . . . it seemed like a good idea at the time. *Journal of Educational Change, 17*, 529–537.

Epstein, J. L. (2010). School/family/community partnerships: Caring for the children we share. *Phi Delta Kappan, 92*, 81–96.

Epstein, J. L., Sanders, M. G., Sheldon, S. B., Simon, B. S., Salinas, K. C., Jansorn, N. R., Van Voorhis, F. L., . . . Williams, K. J. (2009). *School, family, and community partnership: Your handbook for action* (3rd. ed.). Thousand Oaks, CA: Corwin.

Florida, R. (2017). *The new urban crisis*. New York, NY: Basic Books.

Fraser, B. J. (2012). *Classroom environment*. New York, NY: Routledge.

Freire, P. (1974). *Education for critical consciousness*. London, UK: Bloomsbury.

Freire, P. (2000). *Pedagogy of the oppressed*. New York, NY: Bloomsbury.

Freire, P. (2013). *Education for critical consciousness*. London, UK: Bloomsbury Academic.

Fromm, E. (1941). *Escape from freedom*. New York, NY: Farrar & Rinehart.

Fromm, E. (1969). *Escape from freedom* (2nd ed.). New York, NY: Holt.

Fullan, M. (2014). *The principal: Three keys for maximizing impact*. San Francisco, CA: Jossey-Bass

Fullan, M. (2015). *Freedom to change*. San Francisco, CA: Jossey-Bass.

Fullan, M. (2017). *Indelible leadership: Always leave them learning*. Thousand Oaks, CA: Corwin.

Fullan, M., & Edwards, M. (2017). *The power of unstoppable momentum: Key drivers to revolutionize your district.* Bloomington, IN: Solution Tree.

Fullan, M., & Gallagher, M. J. (2017). *Transforming systems: Deep learning and the equity hypothesis.* Palo Alto, CA: Learning Policy Institute.

Fullan, M., & Hargreaves, A. (2016). *Bringing the profession back.* Oxford, OH: Learning Forward.

Fullan, M., & Quinn, J. (2016). *Coherence: The right drivers in action for schools, districts, and systems.* Thousand Oaks, CA: Corwin.

Gallup. (2016). 2016 Gallup Student Poll: A snapshot of results and findings. Retrieved from http://www.gallup.com/file/reports/211025/2016 Gallup Student Poll Snapshot Report.pdf

Grey, A. (2016). The 10 skills you need to thrive in the fourth industrial revolution. *World Economic Forum.* Retrieved from https://www.weforum.org/agenda/2016/01/the-10-skills-you-need-to-thrive-in-the-fourth-industrial-revolution

Hattie, J. (2012). *Visible learning for teachers.* New York, NY: Routledge.

Heller, R., & Wolfe, R. (2015). *Effective schools for deeper learning: An exploratory study. Students at the center: Deeper learning research series.* Boston, MA: Jobs for the Future.

Helm, H., Beneke, S., & Steinheimer, K. (2007). *Windows on learning: Documenting young children's work.* Ann Arbor, MI: Teachers College Press.

Howcroft, J. (2016). *What makes a great community?* [NPDL Exemplar].

Huberman, M., Bitter, C., Anthony, J., & O'Day, J. (2014). *The shape of deeper learning: Strategies, structures, and cultures in deeper learning network high schools. Report #1 findings from the study of deeper learning: Opportunities and outcomes.* Washington, DC: American Institutes for Research. Retrieved from http://www.air.org/sites/default/files/downloads/report/Report%201%20The%20Shape%20of%20Deeper%20Learning_9–23–14v2.pdf

Hutchins, D. J., Greenfeld, M. G., Epstein, J. L., Sanders, M. G., & Galindo, C. (2012). *Multicultural partnerships: Involve all families.* New York, NY: Taylor and Francis.

Ilo, A., & Saarenkunnas, M. (2016). *Europe.* [NPDL Exemplar].

Institute for the Future for University of Phoenix Research Institute. (2011). Future work skills 2020. Retrieved from http://www.iftf.org/uploads/media/SR-1382A_UPRI_future_work_skills_sm.pdf

The Internet challenge in China: A case study of Tencent. (2015). [Seminar]. Palo Alto, CA: Stanford Law School.

Jenkins, L. (2013). *Permission to forget.* Milwaukee, WI: American Society for Quality.

Jenkins, L. (2015). *Optimize your school: It's all about strategy.* Thousand Oaks, CA: Corwin.

Kluger, J. (2009). *Simplexity: Why simple things become complex (and how complex things can be made simple).* New York, NY: Hyperion.

Lindstrom, M. (2016). *Small data: The tiny clues that uncover huge trends.* New York, NY: St. Martin's Press.

McAfee, A., & Brynjolfsson, E. (2017). *Harnessing the digital world: Machine platform crowd.* New York, NY: W. W. Norton.

Mehta, J. (2016, August 25). Deeper learning: 10 ways you can die. [Web log comment]. Retrieved from http://blogs.edweek.org/edweek/learning_deeply/2016/08/deeper_learning_10_ways_you_can_die.html

Mehta, J., & Fine, S. (2015). *The why, what, where, and how of deeper learning in American secondary schools. Students at the center: Deeper learning research series*. Boston, MA: Jobs for the Future.

Miller, P. [millerpEDU]. (2017, February 7). The modern learning "space" includes physical and virtual spaces but more importantly the cultural and relationship spaces. #innovations21 [Tweet]. Retrieved from https://twitter.com/millerpEDU/status/828980776502964228

Montessori, M. (2013). *The Montessori method*. Piscataway, NJ: Transaction.

Moore, G. (1965). Cramming more components onto integrated circuits. *Electronics*, 114–117.

New Pedagogies for Deep Learning. (2016). NPDL Global Report. (1st ed.). Ontario, Canada: Fullan, M., McEachen, J., Quinn, J. Retrieved from http://npdl.global/wp-content/uploads/2016/12/npdl-global-report-2016.pdf

New Pedagogies for Deep Learning: A Global Partnership. (2016). *Bendigo Senior Secondary College speed dating with the pollies*. Retrieved from http://fuse.education.vic.gov.au/?8KKQKL

Noguera, P., Darling-Hammond, L., & Friedlaender, D. (2015). *Equal opportunity for deeper learning. Students at the center: Deeper learning research series*. Boston, MA: Jobs for the Future.

OECD. (2016). *Global competency for an inclusive world*. Paris, France: OECD.

Ontario Ministry of Education. (2014a). *Achieving excellence: A renewed vision for education in Ontario*. Ontario, Canada: Author. Retrieved from http://www.edu.gov.on.ca/eng/about/renewedvision.pdf

Ontario Ministry of Education. (2014b). *Capacity building series: Collaborative inquiry in Ontario*. Ontario, Canada: Author. Retrieved from http://www.edu.gov.on.ca/eng/literacynumeracy/inspire/research/CBS_CollaborativeInquiry.pdf

Ontario Ministry of Education. (2014c). *How does learning happen? Ontario's pedagogy for the early years*. Ontario, Canada: Author. Retrieved from http://www.edu.gov.on.ca/childcare/HowLearningHappens.pdf

Ontario Ministry of Education. (2016). *Ontario's well-being strategy for education*. Ontario, Canada: Author. Retrieved from http://www.edu.gov.on.ca/eng/about/WBDiscussionDocument.pdf

OWP/P Cannon Design Inc., VS Furniture, & Bruce Mau Design. (2010). *The third teacher: 79 ways you can use design to transform teaching & learning*. New York, NY: Abrams.

Pane, J., Steiner, E., Baird, M., Hamilton. L., & Pane, J. (2017). *Informing progress: Insights on personalized learning implementation and effects*. Santa Monica, CA: Rand Corporation; Funded by Bill and Melinda Gates Foundation.

Pappert, S. (1994). *The children's machine: Rethinking school in the age of the computer*. New York, NY: Basic Books.

Piaget, J. (1966). *The origin of intelligence in the child*. London, UK: Routledge & Keegan Paul.

Quaglia, R., & Corso, M. (2014). *Student voice: The instrument of change*. Thousand Oaks, CA: Corwin.

Ramo, J. C. (2016). *The seventh sense*. New York, NY: Little Brown.

Robinson, K. (2015). *Creative schools*. New York, NY: Viking.

Robinson, V. (2017). *Reduce change to increase improvement*. Thousand Oaks, CA: Corwin.

Rubin, C. M. (2016). The global search for education: Would small data mean big change? [Blog]. Retrieved from http://www.huffingtonpost.com/c-m-rubin/the-global-search-for-edu_b_12983592.html

Ryan, R. M., & Deci, E. L. (2017). *Self-determination theory: Basic psychological needs in motivation, development, and wellness.* New York, NY: Guilford.

Schein, E. H. (2010). *Organizational culture and leadership* (4th ed.). San Francisco, CA: Jossey-Bass.

Scott, G. (2016). *Transforming graduate capabilities & achievement standards for a sustainable future.* Sydney, Australia: Western Sydney University.

Scott, K. (2017). *Radical candor.* New York, NY: St. Martin's Press.

Shnur, J. (2016). Pine River Annual Improvement Plan 2017, personal communication, December 2016.

Tijssen, R., & Yegros, A. (2016). The most innovative universities: An alternative approach to ranking. *Times Higher Education.* Retrieved from https://www.timeshighereducation.com/blog/most-innovative-universities-alternative-approach-ranking

Timperley, H. (2011). *The power of professional learning.* Maidenhead, UK: Open University Press.

Tough, P. (2016). *Helping children succeed: What works and why.* New York, NY: Houghton Mifflin Harcourt.

Walker, B., & Soule, S. (2017, June 20). Changing company culture requires a movement, not a mandate. *Harvard Business Review,* 2–6.

Index

Acknowledgments

When you conduct a global partnership involving hundreds of schools over almost 5 years, you have thousands of people to thank. We have this in spades, and we can say that our cardinal rule of learning holds up well, namely that *80% of our best ideas come from leading practitioners*. We find these people in schools, districts, municipalities, governments, and more. We thank these co-learners of all ages for what we have learned together.

We thank the Hewlett Foundation, particularly Barbara Chow and Marc Chun for their decadelong commitment to deep learning and for their unequivocal support. To the Stuart Foundation for their long-term funding of our work in System Change in California, and for their comprehensive leadership when it comes to deep system change.

We are blessed with committed quality all around us, the country and cluster leaders in each country: Lynn Davie, Mary Coverdale, Ben Wilson (Australia); Tom D'Amico, Anita Simpson, Dana Liebermann, Bill Hogarth, Patrick Miller (Canada); Vesa Åyrås, Kati Tiainen, Kaisa Jussila, Paula Vorne (Finland), Marlou van Beek, Baukje Bemener (Netherlands); Derek Wenmoth, Margot McKeegan (New Zealand); Miguel Brechner, Claudia Brovetto, and Andrés Peri (Uruguay); and Larry Thomas, Pam Estvold, JoDee Marcellin (United States). Thanks to the scores of schools, teachers, and administrators who contributed their stories in exemplars and videos.

Then our global team, a powerhouse of dedicated leaders: Mag Gardner, Max Drummy, Cecilia de la Paz, Bill Hogarth, Catie Schuster, and Matt Kane. We work with a host of thought leaders on various initiatives: Eleanor Adam, Santiago Rincón-Gallardo, Jean Clinton, MaryJean Gallagher, Peter Hill, Bill Hogarth, Cathy Montreuil, John Malloy, Joelle Rodway, Andreas Schleicher, Michael Stevenson, Andy Hargreaves, Carol Campbell, and more.

There has been great support for the production of this book. Our own team shines with quality: Claudia Cuttress, Mary Meucci, and on graphics Trudy Lane and Nolan Hellyer. We thank the Ontario Principals' Council for their longstanding support, and co-publication of all of our work. Finally, to our fabulous publisher, Corwin: fast, flexible, and fastidious about quality. Arnis, Desirée, Melanie, Deanna, and the Corwin infrastructure, we can't thank you enough.

About the Authors

Michael Fullan, OC, is the former Dean of the Ontario Institute for Studies in Education of the University of Toronto. Recognized as a worldwide authority on educational reform, he advises policy makers and local leaders around the world in helping to achieve the moral purpose of all children learning. Michael Fullan received the Order of Canada in December 2012. He holds five honorary doctorates from universities around the world.

Michael is a prolific, award-winning author whose books have been published in many languages. His book *Leading in a Culture of Change* was awarded the 2002 Book of the Year Award by Learning Forward (formerly the National Staff Development Council), *Breakthrough* (with Peter Hill and Carmel Crévola) won the 2006 Book of the Year Award from the American Association of Colleges for Teacher Education (AACTE), and *Turnaround Leadership in Higher Education* (with Geoff Scott) won the Bellwether Book Award in 2009. *Change Wars* (with Andy Hargreaves) was awarded the 2009 Book of the Year Award by Learning Forward, and *Professional Capital* (with Andy Hargreaves) won the AACTE 2013 Book of the Year and was given the Grawemeyer Prize for 2015—an award that recognizes "the power a single creative idea can have on the world." Michael Fullan's latest books are *The Principal: Three Keys for Maximizing Impact, Coherence: Putting the Right Drivers in Action* (with Joanne Quinn), *Indelible Leadership: Always Leave Them Learning,* and *The Power of Unstoppable Momentum* (with Mark Edwards). He currently serves as an advisor to the premier and minister of education in Ontario.

Joanne Quinn is an international consultant, author, and speaker and leads her own consulting firm focused on whole system change, capacity building, learning, and leadership. She is a cofounder and Global Director of New Pedagogies for Deep Learning, a global partnership focused on transforming learning. Joanne consults with governments, foundations, and education systems and leads whole system change projects at the state, province, national, and global levels. Joanne has provided leadership at all levels of education as a Superintendent of Education, Implementation Advisor to the Ontario Ministry of Education, and Director of Continuing Education at the University of Toronto. Joanne is past president of Learning Forward and founding president of the Ontario affiliate.

Her recent books include the best-sellers *Coherence: The Right Drivers in Action for Schools, Districts, and Systems* with Michael Fullan and *The Taking Action Guide for Building Coherence in Schools, Districts, and Systems* with Michael Fullan and Eleanor Adam. Joanne's diverse leadership roles and her passion to open windows of opportunity for all give her a unique perspective on influencing positive change.

Joanne McEachen is an internationally recognized education leader who serves as the Global New Measures Director for New Pedagogies for Deep Learning (NPDL), cofounded and in partnership with Michael Fullan and Joanne Quinn.

Joanne is also the CEO and founder of The Learner First. Her work with The Learner First frames global lessons learned throughout her experience in education over the past 30 years and through the NPDL partnership in the context of the United States, revolutionizing measurement, assessment, teaching, and learning through the lens of whole system change. Her methodology interrogates the system through the eyes of the least-served learners, embracing and celebrating their cultural identities and individual interests and needs.

Joanne's expertise spans every layer of the education system. She has been a teacher, principal, regional manager (superintendent), and a national and whole system change leader in New Zealand and around the world. With firsthand experience addressing the issues faced by schools, districts, and education departments, Joanne provides tools, processes, measures, and thinking that, combined with leveraging digital technologies, deepen learning for every learner.

CORWIN LEADERSHIP

Simon T. Bailey & Marceta F. Reilly
On providing a simple, sustainable framework that will help you move your school from mediocrity to brilliance.

Edie L. Holcomb
Use data to construct an equitable learning environment, develop instruction, and empower effective PL communities.

Debbie Silver & Dedra Stafford
Equip educators to develop resilient and mindful learners primed for academic growth and personal success.

Peter Gamwell & Jane Daly
A fresh perspective on how to nurture creativity, innovation, leadership, and engagement.

Steven Katz, Lisa Ain Dack, & John Malloy
Leverage the oppositional forces of top-down expectations and bottom-up experience to create an intelligent, responsive school.

Lyn Sharratt & Beate Planche
A resource-rich guide that provides a strategic path to achieving sustainable communities of deep learners.

Peter M. DeWitt
Meet stakeholders where they are, motivate them to improve, and model how to do it.

Leadership that Makes an Impact

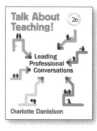

Charlotte Danielson
Harness the power of informal professional conversation and invite teachers to boost achievement.

Liz Wiseman, Lois Allen, & Elise Foster
Use leadership to bring out the best in others—liberating staff to excel and doubling your team's effectiveness.

Eric Sheninger
Use digital resources to create a new school culture, increase engagement, and facilitate real-time PD.

Russell J. Quaglia, Michael J. Corso, & Lisa L. Lande
Listen to your school's voice to see how you can increase engagement, involvement, and academic motivation.

Michael Fullan, Joanne Quinn, & Joanne McEachen
Learn the right drivers to mobilize complex, coherent, whole-system change and transform learning for all students.

CORWIN
LEADERSHIP

A SAGE Publishing Company

Helping educators make the greatest impact

CORWIN HAS ONE MISSION: to enhance education through intentional professional learning.

We build long-term relationships with our authors, educators, clients, and associations who partner with us to develop and continuously improve the best evidence-based practices that establish and support lifelong learning.

The Ontario Principals' Council (OPC) is a voluntary professional association representing 5,000 practising school leaders in elementary and secondary schools across Ontario. We believe that exemplary leadership results in outstanding schools and improved student achievement. We foster quality leadership through world-class professional services and supports, striving to continuously achieve **"quality leadership—our principal product."**